DIRT TO DOLLARS

Your Comprehensive Guide to Starting a Successful Cleaning Business

EmptyInkwell

Copyright © 2024 EmptyInkwell

All rights reserved

ISBN: 9798324225599

Chapter 1: Introduction

Welcome to your comprehensive guide to starting and operating a successful cleaning business. This book is designed to be a valuable resource for individuals who are eager to venture into the cleaning industry. Our aim is to provide you with step-by-step instructions, practical tips, and insightful strategies to help you navigate your entrepreneurial journey.

The cleaning industry is a vibrant and essential sector, offering a plethora of opportunities for entrepreneurs. It encompasses a wide range of services, from residential cleaning to commercial cleaning, and specialized cleaning services like carpet cleaning, window cleaning, and more. This industry thrives on the fundamental human need for cleanliness and order, a need that transcends economic fluctuations and societal changes.

The purpose of this book is to equip you with the necessary knowledge and tools to start your own cleaning business. Starting a business can be a challenging endeavor, filled with uncertainties and risks. However, with the right guidance and resources, it can also be an exciting journey that leads to financial success and personal fulfillment.

We have structured this book to be a practical, easy-to-follow guide that will walk you through the entire process, from conceptualizing your business idea to managing your day-to-day operations. Each chapter is designed to provide in-depth information and actionable steps that you can apply directly to your business.

In the following chapters, we will cover a wide range of topics that are crucial to the success of your cleaning business. These include understanding the cleaning industry, developing a business plan, navigating legalities and licenses, sourcing equipment and supplies, hiring and training staff, marketing and customer acquisition, pricing and contracts, customer service and retention, and strategies for growth and expansion.

Each chapter is meticulously designed to provide detailed insights into each aspect of running a cleaning business. We will delve into the specifics, provide practical examples, and offer actionable tips that you can implement in your own business. Our goal is to provide you with a comprehensive understanding of each topic, enabling you to make informed decisions as you start and grow your cleaning business.

This book is designed to be a resource that you can refer to at any stage of your business journey. Whether you're just starting out or looking to grow your existing cleaning business, you'll find valuable insights and strategies in each chapter. We recommend reading the book in order, as each chapter builds on the concepts introduced in the previous ones. However, feel free to jump to specific chapters that are most relevant to your current needs. The book is structured in a way that allows for flexibility, enabling you to use it in a way that best suits your learning style and business needs.

Starting a cleaning business can be a rewarding and profitable venture. With the right guidance, resources, and determination, you can build a successful business that provides valuable services to your clients and contributes positively to your community. We hope that this book will serve as a helpful guide on your entrepreneurial journey. As you embark on this exciting journey, remember that success comes to those who are prepared, adaptable, and resilient.

Importance of cleanliness & industry opportunities

Cleanliness, as an essential aspect of human life, holds a significant place in our daily routines, our culture, and our collective consciousness. It is not just about maintaining an aesthetically pleasing environment; it's about promoting health, preventing disease, and creating a positive atmosphere. Cleanliness is fundamental to our physical well-being and our mental peace. It is a universal need that transcends geographical boundaries, cultural differences, and social statuses.

In the context of a business environment, cleanliness takes on an even greater significance. A clean workplace boosts employee productivity, which creates a positive impression on clients and complies with health and safety regulations. Similarly, a clean home enhances the quality of life, provides a safe space for families, and contributes to overall happiness and comfort.

This universal need for cleanliness presents a vast array of opportunities in the cleaning industry. The industry is as diverse as the cleaning needs of individuals and businesses, offering services ranging from residential cleaning, commercial cleaning, to specialized cleaning services.

Residential cleaning services cater to homes, apartments, and residential complexes. They include regular cleaning tasks like dusting, vacuuming, mopping, bathroom cleaning, kitchen cleaning, and more. With the fast-paced modern lifestyle, many families prefer hiring professional cleaning services to maintain their homes, providing a steady market for residential cleaning.

Commercial cleaning services cater to businesses, offices, retail stores, restaurants, hotels, and other commercial establishments. These services are crucial for maintaining a clean, healthy, and attractive business environment. Commercial cleaning often requires a higher level of expertise and more specialized equipment than residential cleaning, offering an opportunity for cleaning businesses to provide value-added services.

Specialized cleaning services focus on specific cleaning needs that require specialized skills or equipment. These include window cleaning, carpet cleaning, industrial cleaning, post-construction cleaning, and more. Specialized cleaning services often cater to niche markets, providing ample opportunities for businesses to differentiate themselves and cater to specific customer needs.

The cleaning industry also presents opportunities for innovation and growth. With increasing awareness about environmental sustainability, there is a growing demand for green cleaning services that use environmentally friendly products and methods. Technological advancements are also creating opportunities for improving efficiency and effectiveness in cleaning services.

The importance of cleanliness in our lives and our society presents numerous opportunities in the cleaning industry. Whether it's providing regular cleaning services to homes and businesses or offering specialized cleaning solutions, there are myriad ways to create a successful business in this industry.

The challenges of starting a business & how this book can help

Embarking on the journey of starting a business is an exciting endeavor filled with possibilities. However, it's also a path laden with challenges that test your resolve, adaptability, and resilience. In the context of starting a cleaning business, these challenges can range from operational to strategic, each requiring a unique set of skills and knowledge to overcome.

One of the first challenges budding entrepreneurs face is the development of a clear and viable business idea. This involves identifying the type of cleaning services you intend to offer, understanding your target customers, and defining what sets your business apart from the competition. It requires a deep understanding of the cleaning industry, market trends, and the specific needs of your potential clients. Without a clear business idea, you risk entering the market without a unique value proposition, making it difficult to attract and retain customers.

Creating a comprehensive business plan is another significant challenge. A business plan serves as a roadmap for your business, outlining your business goals, strategies for achieving these goals, and the metrics for measuring your progress. It requires careful planning, market research, and financial forecasting. Without a well-crafted business plan, you may find it difficult to secure funding, attract investors, or guide your business towards growth and profitability.

Navigating the legalities of starting a business is another hurdle. This includes registering your business, obtaining the necessary licenses and permits, and understanding and complying with industry regulations. Legal missteps can lead to penalties, damage your reputation, and even lead to the closure of your business.

Operational challenges include finding and retaining reliable staff, investing in quality equipment and supplies, and managing day-to-day operations. The cleaning industry is labor-intensive, and finding staff who are reliable, skilled, and hardworking is crucial. Additionally, investing in high-quality equipment and supplies can significantly impact the quality of your cleaning services.

Marketing your business and acquiring customers is another challenge that cleaning businesses face. With the cleaning industry being highly competitive, standing out from the competition and attracting customers requires effective marketing strategies. This includes leveraging both traditional and digital marketing channels, creating a strong brand, and delivering excellent customer service.

Despite these challenges, starting a cleaning business can be a rewarding and profitable venture. And this is where this book comes in. This book is designed to guide you through these challenges and equip you with the knowledge and tools you need to start and operate a successful cleaning business.

Each chapter of this book delves into a specific aspect of starting a cleaning business, providing in-depth information, practical tips, and actionable steps. From understanding the cleaning industry and developing a business plan to navigating legalities, sourcing equipment, hiring staff, and marketing your business, this book covers it all.

By reading this book, you'll gain a comprehensive understanding of what it takes to start a cleaning business. You'll learn about the opportunities and challenges in the cleaning industry, the steps involved in starting a business, and the strategies for growing and sustaining your business. This book is not just about providing information; it's about empowering you to make informed decisions, solve problems, and turn your entrepreneurial dream into reality.

As you embark on this exciting journey, remember that every challenge is an opportunity for learning and growth. With determination, resilience, and the right guidance, you can overcome the challenges, build a successful cleaning business, and achieve your entrepreneurial dreams. Let's get started on this journey towards starting and operating a successful cleaning business.

Chapter Overview

As we conclude the introductory chapter of this comprehensive guide to starting and operating a successful cleaning business, let's take a moment to preview the journey ahead. Each subsequent chapter of this book is designed to delve into a specific aspect of the cleaning business, providing you with in-depth knowledge, practical insights, and actionable strategies.

In **Chapter 2: Understanding the Cleaning Industry**, we will explore the landscape of the cleaning industry. We will discuss the different types of cleaning services, the current market trends, and the competitive landscape. This chapter will provide you with a solid understanding of the industry you are about to enter, helping you identify opportunities and challenges.

Chapter 3: Developing Your Business Plan will guide you through the process of creating a comprehensive business plan. From defining your business objectives and understanding your target market to planning your marketing and sales strategy and financial projections, this chapter will equip you with a roadmap for your entrepreneurial journey.

In **Chapter 4: Legalities and Licenses**, we will navigate the legal aspects of starting a cleaning business. We will cover topics like business registration, obtaining necessary licenses and permits, and understanding industry regulations. This chapter will ensure that you are well-prepared to meet all legal requirements and operate your business with confidence.

Chapter 5: Equipment and Supplies will provide information on the equipment and supplies needed to operate a cleaning business. From sourcing these resources effectively to managing them efficiently, this chapter will guide you through all aspects of handling your business's physical resources.

In **Chapter 6: Hiring and Training Staff**, we will focus on the human resource aspect of the business. From hiring practices and staff training to employee management and maintaining a healthy work environment, this chapter will equip you with the skills and knowledge to build and manage a strong team.

Chapter 7: Marketing and Customer Acquisition will provide strategies for marketing your business and acquiring customers. We will cover both traditional and digital marketing channels and provide tips on attracting and retaining customers.

In **Chapter 8: Pricing and Contracts**, we will guide you on how to price your services competitively and manage contracts effectively. We will discuss different pricing strategies and provide tips on negotiating contracts and managing client relationships.

Chapter 9: Customer Service and Retention will emphasize the importance of customer service and discuss strategies for customer retention. From handling customer complaints and improving customer satisfaction to building customer loyalty, this chapter will ensure that you are well-equipped to deliver excellent customer service.

Chapter 10: Growth and Expansion will discuss strategies for growing and expanding your business. From scaling operations and exploring new markets to continuous improvement and sustaining success, this chapter will guide you through the various stages of business growth.

In addition to these chapters, we have also included five additional chapters that cover more specific aspects of running a cleaning business. These chapters include **Chapter 11: Sustainability in the Cleaning Industry**, **Chapter 12: Technology in the Cleaning Industry**, **Chapter 13: Health and Safety Considerations**, **Chapter 14: Building a Brand**, and **Chapter 15: Dealing with Challenges and Setbacks**.

Each of these chapters is designed to provide detailed insights into a specific aspect of running a cleaning business. They will delve into the specifics, provide practical examples, and offer actionable tips that you can implement in your own business.

As you progress through this book, you will gain a comprehensive understanding of what it takes to start and operate a successful cleaning business. You will learn about the opportunities and challenges in the cleaning industry, the steps involved in starting a business, and the strategies for growing and sustaining your business.

Chapter 2: Understanding the Cleaning Industry

The cleaning industry is a vast and diverse sector that plays a crucial role in maintaining cleanliness, hygiene, and aesthetic appeal in various settings. It encompasses a wide range of services, from residential cleaning and commercial cleaning to specialized cleaning services such as window cleaning, carpet cleaning, and industrial cleaning. This industry caters to a broad spectrum of clients, including homeowners, businesses, schools, hospitals, and government agencies, among others.

The significance of the cleaning industry cannot be overstated. Cleanliness is not just about maintaining an aesthetically pleasing environment; it's about promoting health, preventing disease, and enhancing the quality of life. In a business setting, a clean and well-maintained environment can boost employee productivity, create a positive impression on clients and visitors, and comply with health and safety regulations. In a residential setting, a clean home can enhance the quality of life, provide a safe and comfortable living space, and contribute to the overall well-being of the residents.

The cleaning industry is also a significant contributor to the economy. It provides employment opportunities for millions of people worldwide and generates billions of dollars in revenue each year. The industry is characterized by low entry barriers, making it an attractive option for entrepreneurs and small businesses. With the right skills, knowledge, and resources, anyone can start a cleaning business and grow it into a successful venture.

Despite its significance, the cleaning industry is often overlooked and undervalued. Cleaning is sometimes seen as a mundane and unglamorous task. However, the reality is that cleaning professionals perform a vital service that contributes to our health, well-being, and quality of life. They work behind the scenes to ensure that our homes, workplaces, and public spaces are clean, safe, and pleasant to be in.

The cleaning industry is also evolving and adapting to changing consumer needs and market trends. With increasing awareness about environmental sustainability, there is a growing demand for green cleaning services that use environmentally friendly products and methods. Technological advancements are also transforming the industry, with the introduction of automated cleaning machines, digital booking platforms, and other innovative solutions.

Furthermore, the COVID-19 pandemic has underscored the importance of cleanliness and hygiene in preventing the spread of disease. It has highlighted the crucial role of cleaning professionals in maintaining public health and safety. As a result, the cleaning industry has gained increased recognition and respect, and the demand for cleaning services has surged.

The cleaning industry is a vital and dynamic sector that offers numerous opportunities for entrepreneurs. Whether you're planning to start a residential cleaning service, a commercial cleaning business, or a specialized cleaning company, understanding the cleaning industry is the first step towards success.

Types of cleaning services & their demand

The cleaning industry is a diverse sector that offers a wide range of services to cater to the varied needs of its clientele. These services can be broadly categorized into residential cleaning services, commercial cleaning services, and specialized cleaning services. Each of these categories has its own unique characteristics, demands, and opportunities.

Residential Cleaning Services

Residential cleaning services cater to homes, apartments, and other residential spaces. These services typically include regular cleaning tasks such as dusting, vacuuming, mopping, bathroom cleaning, and kitchen cleaning. Some residential cleaning companies also offer additional services like deep cleaning, move-in/move-out cleaning, and seasonal cleaning.

The demand for residential cleaning services has been on the rise, driven by factors such as increasing urbanization, dual-income households, and a growing preference for professional cleaning services. With the fast-paced modern lifestyle, many families prefer hiring professional cleaning services to maintain their homes, providing a steady market for residential cleaning.

Commercial Cleaning Services

Commercial cleaning services cater to businesses, offices, retail stores, restaurants, hotels, and other commercial establishments. These services are crucial for maintaining a clean, healthy, and attractive business environment. Commercial cleaning often requires a higher level of expertise and more specialized equipment than residential cleaning.

The demand for commercial cleaning services is largely driven by the growth of the commercial sector. Businesses understand the importance of a clean and well-maintained environment in enhancing productivity, creating a positive impression on clients, and complying with health and safety regulations. As a result, they are willing to invest in professional cleaning services, creating ample opportunities for commercial cleaning businesses.

Specialized Cleaning Services

Specialized cleaning services focus on specific cleaning needs that require specialized skills or equipment. These include window cleaning, carpet cleaning, industrial cleaning, post-construction cleaning, and more. Specialized cleaning services often cater to niche markets, providing ample opportunities for businesses to differentiate themselves and cater to specific customer needs.

The demand for specialized cleaning services is driven by the need for expert cleaning solutions. Whether it's cleaning high-rise windows, maintaining industrial machinery, or cleaning carpets, clients prefer professionals who have the skills and equipment to do the job effectively and safely.

The cleaning industry, with its diverse range of services, caters to a wide array of cleaning needs. Whether it's a homeowner looking for a reliable cleaning service, a business needing to maintain a clean and healthy environment, or a construction company requiring post-construction cleanup, the cleaning industry has a solution.

Market trends & future industry prospects

Understanding the current market trends and future prospects is crucial for any business, and the cleaning industry is no exception. These trends provide insights into the evolving needs and preferences of customers, emerging technologies, and changes in the regulatory environment. They help businesses stay relevant, competitive, and profitable in the long run.

Current Market Trends in the Cleaning Industry

1. **Green Cleaning**: With increasing awareness about environmental sustainability, there is a growing trend towards green cleaning. More and more customers are preferring cleaning services that use environmentally friendly products and practices. This trend is driven by the increasing awareness about the harmful effects of certain cleaning chemicals on the environment and human health.
2. **Technological Advancements**: The cleaning industry is increasingly leveraging technology

to improve efficiency and effectiveness. From automated cleaning machines and advanced cleaning solutions to digital platforms for booking and managing cleaning services, technology is transforming the way cleaning services are delivered.
3. **Specialized Cleaning Services**: There is a growing demand for specialized cleaning services that cater to specific cleaning needs. These include services like window cleaning, carpet cleaning, industrial cleaning, and post-construction cleaning. As customers seek high-quality, professional cleaning solutions, businesses offering specialized cleaning services are witnessing growth.
4. **Home Sanitization and Disinfection Services**: The COVID-19 pandemic has underscored the importance of cleanliness and hygiene in preventing the spread of diseases. This has led to a surge in demand for home sanitization and disinfection services. Cleaning businesses that offer these services have seen significant growth in the past year.

Future Prospects in the Cleaning Industry

The future of the cleaning industry looks promising, with several opportunities for growth and expansion.
1. **Continued Demand for Green Cleaning**: The trend towards green cleaning is expected to continue in the future. As customers become more environmentally conscious, the demand for cleaning services that use eco-friendly products and practices is likely to increase.

2. **Increased Use of Technology:** The use of technology in the cleaning industry is expected to increase in the future. Technological advancements like AI, IoT, and robotics have the potential to revolutionize the cleaning industry, making cleaning services more efficient, effective, and customer-friendly.
3. **Growth in Specialized Cleaning Services:** The demand for specialized cleaning services is expected to grow in the future. As customers seek professional, high-quality cleaning solutions, businesses offering specialized cleaning services are likely to witness growth.
4. **Increased Focus on Health and Hygiene:** The COVID-19 pandemic has brought health and hygiene to the forefront. This increased focus on cleanliness and hygiene is expected to continue in the future, driving demand for professional cleaning services.

The cleaning industry is a dynamic and evolving sector with numerous opportunities for growth and expansion. By understanding the current market trends and future prospects, businesses can position themselves for success in this industry.

Positioning your business in a competitive landscape

The cleaning industry, like any other industry, is characterized by a competitive landscape. Businesses compete on various fronts, including the quality of services, pricing, customer service, and brand reputation. Understanding the competitive landscape is crucial for positioning your business effectively and gaining a competitive edge.

The Competitive Landscape of the Cleaning Industry

The cleaning industry is highly fragmented, with numerous small and medium-sized businesses competing alongside large corporations. These businesses offer a wide range of services, from general cleaning services to specialized cleaning services. The competition is fierce, and businesses need to differentiate themselves to stand out and attract customers.

In the residential cleaning segment, competition is primarily based on price, quality of service, and customer service. Businesses that offer high-quality services at competitive prices and provide excellent customer service tend to attract more customers. Additionally, businesses that offer specialized services, such as green cleaning or deep cleaning, can differentiate themselves and attract a niche market.

In the commercial cleaning segment, competition is more complex. Businesses not only compete on price, quality, and customer service, but also on their ability to meet the specific needs of commercial clients. For instance, a commercial client may require cleaning services outside of regular business hours, or they may require specialized cleaning services for industrial equipment. Businesses that can meet these specific needs can gain a competitive edge.

Positioning Your Cleaning Business

Positioning your cleaning business involves defining how you want your business to be perceived by your target customers. It involves identifying your unique value proposition – what sets your business apart from the competition – and communicating this to your target customers.

Here are some strategies to position your cleaning business effectively:

1. **Identify Your Unique Value Proposition**: What makes your cleaning business unique? Do you offer specialized cleaning services? Do you use environmentally friendly cleaning products? Do you provide exceptional customer service? Identifying what sets your business apart from the competition is the first step in positioning your business.
2. **Understand Your Target Customers**: Who are your target customers? What are their cleaning needs? What are their preferences? Understanding your target customers will help you tailor your services to meet their needs and preferences, thereby attracting and retaining more customers.
3. **Communicate Your Value Proposition**: Once you've identified your unique value proposition and understood your target customers, the next step is to communicate your value proposition to your target customers. This can be done through various marketing channels, such as your website, social media, advertising, and word-of-mouth.

4. **Deliver on Your Promise**: Positioning your business is not just about making promises; it's about delivering on those promises. Ensure that you deliver the high-quality services that you promise to your customers. This will not only satisfy your customers but also enhance your business's reputation and attract more customers.

Understanding the competitive landscape and positioning your business effectively is crucial for success in the cleaning industry. By differentiating your business, understanding your target customers, communicating your value proposition, and delivering on your promise, you can gain a competitive edge and grow your cleaning business.

Chapter 3: Developing Your Business Plan

A business plan is a fundamental tool for any entrepreneur. It serves as a roadmap, guiding you through the process of starting and operating your business. It outlines your business goals, strategies for achieving these goals, and the metrics for measuring your progress. A well-crafted business plan can help you attract investors, secure funding, and guide your business towards growth and profitability.

The Importance of a Business Plan

The importance of a business plan cannot be overstated. It provides a clear direction for your business, helping you make informed decisions and avoid costly mistakes. It helps you identify your target market, understand your competition, and develop effective marketing and sales strategies. It also helps you plan your financials, including your revenue model, cost structure, and financial projections.

A business plan is not just a document; it's a strategic tool that helps you navigate the complexities of starting and running a business. It forces you to think critically about your business idea, evaluate its feasibility, and plan for its implementation. It helps you identify potential challenges and devise strategies to overcome them. It also helps you track your progress and make necessary adjustments as your business grows and evolves.

Moreover, a business plan is a crucial tool for communicating your business idea to potential investors, lenders, and partners. It helps them understand your business, assess its potential, and make informed decisions about investing in your business. A well-crafted business plan can help you gain the trust and support of these stakeholders, thereby increasing your chances of securing the necessary funding and resources for your business.

Key Components of a Business Plan

A comprehensive business plan typically includes the following key components:
1. **Executive Summary**: This is a brief overview of your business plan. It provides a snapshot of your business, including your business name, location, the products or services you offer, and your plans for growth.
2. **Company Description**: This section provides detailed information about your business. It includes your business structure, ownership, the nature of your business, and the specific needs that your products or services fulfill.
3. **Market Analysis**: This section requires you to conduct detailed research on your industry, target market, and competitors. It helps you understand the market trends, customer needs, and competitive landscape.
4. **Organization and Management**: This section outlines your business's organizational structure and management team. It includes information about the ownership of your business, your team, and their roles.
5. **Services or Products**: This section describes your products or services in detail. It explains what you sell, how your products or services

benefit your customers, and how they differ from those offered by your competitors.
6. **Marketing and Sales Strategy**: This section outlines your strategies for attracting and retaining customers. It covers your marketing plan, sales strategy, and customer service plan.
7. **Funding Request**: If you're seeking funding, this section outlines your current funding requirements, future funding needs over the next five years, how you will use the funds, and the types of funding you would consider.
8. **Financial Projections**: This section provides an overview of your business's financial outlook. It includes projected income statements, balance sheets, cash flow statements, and capital expenditure budgets.
9. **Appendix**: This section includes any additional information that supports your business plan. It can include resumes of key employees, letters of recommendation, patents, job descriptions, contracts, legal information, permits, and other documents.

A business plan is a vital tool for starting and operating a successful cleaning business. It provides a roadmap for your business, helps you make informed decisions, and increases your chances of securing funding.

Define business objectives and understand target market

Defining your business objectives and understanding your target market are two fundamental steps in creating a robust business plan. These elements provide a clear direction for your business and help you focus your efforts on meeting the needs of your customers.

Defining Your Business Objectives

Business objectives are the specific, measurable results that a company plans to achieve over a specific period. They provide a clear direction for the company and serve as a benchmark for measuring progress. Here's how to define your business objectives:

1. **Identify Your Long-Term Goals**: Start by identifying your long-term goals. These are the broad outcomes you want your business to achieve in the long run. For example, you might want to become the leading cleaning service provider in your city or expand your business to other cities.
2. **Set Short-Term Objectives**: Once you have identified your long-term goals, you can set short-term objectives that will help you achieve these goals. These are specific, measurable outcomes that you aim to achieve in the short term. For example, you might set an objective to acquire 100 new customers in the next six months.
3. **Make Your Objectives SMART**: Ensure that your objectives are SMART - Specific, Measurable, Achievable, Relevant, and Time-bound. This means that each objective should clearly define what you want to achieve, how

you will measure your progress, whether it's achievable with the resources you have, whether it's relevant to your long-term goals, and when you aim to achieve it.

Understanding Your Target Market

Your target market is the group of customers that your cleaning business aims to serve. Understanding your target market is crucial for tailoring your services to meet their needs and for developing effective marketing strategies. Here's how to understand your target market:

1. **Identify Your Potential Customers**: Start by identifying who your potential customers are. Are you targeting homeowners, businesses, schools, hospitals, or other establishments? Are you targeting a specific geographical area?
2. **Understand Their Needs and Preferences**: Once you have identified your potential customers, try to understand their cleaning needs and preferences. What types of cleaning services do they require? How often do they require these services? What are their preferences in terms of cleaning products, scheduling, pricing, etc.?
3. **Analyze Your Competition**: Look at other cleaning businesses that are targeting the same market. What services do they offer? How do they price their services? What is their unique selling proposition? Understanding your competition can help you identify gaps in the market that your business can fill.

4. **Segment Your Market**: Depending on the range of services you offer, you might need to segment your market into different groups based on their specific needs and preferences. For example, you might have one segment for residential cleaning services and another for commercial cleaning services. Segmenting your market can help you tailor your services and marketing strategies to each segment.

Defining your business objectives and understanding your target market are crucial steps in developing your business plan. They provide a direction for your business and help you focus your efforts on meeting the needs of your customers.

Marketing & Sales

A well-defined marketing and sales strategy is a critical component of your business plan. It outlines how you intend to attract, convert, and retain customers, which are key to the success and growth of your cleaning business.

Planning Your Marketing Strategy

Your marketing strategy should detail how you plan to communicate your services to your target market. Here are some steps to help you develop an effective marketing strategy:
1. **Define Your Marketing Goals**: Start by outlining what you want to achieve through your marketing efforts. This could be increasing brand awareness, attracting new customers, retaining existing customers, or

increasing sales. Ensure your marketing goals align with your overall business objectives.
2. **Understand Your Target Market**: Identify who your customers are. What are their needs and preferences? What factors influence their decision to hire a cleaning service? Understanding your target market will allow you to tailor your marketing messages to resonate with them.
3. **Choose Your Marketing Channels**: Determine which marketing channels are most effective for reaching your target market. This could include social media, email marketing, content marketing, SEO, print advertising, or even word-of-mouth referrals.
4. **Develop Your Marketing Messages**: Decide on the key messages you want to communicate about your cleaning business. What makes your services unique? Why should customers choose your cleaning service over others? These messages should be consistently communicated across all your marketing channels.
5. **Create a Marketing Budget**: Determine how much you plan to spend on your marketing efforts. This includes the cost of creating marketing materials, advertising, and any other expenses related to marketing.

Planning Your Sales Strategy

Your sales strategy should complement your marketing strategy. It outlines how you will sell your services, convert leads into customers, and achieve

your revenue goals. Here are some steps to help you develop your sales strategy:
1. **Define Your Sales Process**: Outline the steps you will take to sell your services, from initial contact with a potential customer to closing the sale. This could include consultation, quotation, negotiation, and agreement.
2. **Train Your Sales Team**: If you have a team, ensure they are well-trained to sell your services effectively. They should understand your services, your marketing messages, and your sales process.
3. **Manage Customer Relationships**: Develop strategies for building strong relationships with your customers. This could include providing excellent customer service, seeking customer feedback, and offering incentives for repeat business.
4. **Monitor and Adjust Your Sales Strategy**: Regularly review your sales performance and adjust your sales strategy as needed. This could involve trying different sales techniques, targeting different customer segments, or offering new services.

A well-planned marketing and sales strategy can help your cleaning business attract and retain customers, differentiate itself from competitors, and achieve business objectives.

Financial Planning

Financial planning is a cornerstone of your business plan. It provides a clear picture of the financial health of your business, helps you make informed business decisions, and is essential for securing funding or investment. In this section, we will delve into the key components of financial planning, including your revenue model, cost structure, and financial projections.

Revenue Model

The revenue model is a framework that outlines how a business generates income. It identifies the sources of revenue, the value proposition, and the customer segments. For a cleaning business, the revenue model could be based on various factors such as the type of services offered (residential, commercial, specialized), the pricing strategy (hourly rate, flat fee, contract-based), and additional services (deep cleaning, green cleaning).

1. **Type of Services**: The type of cleaning services you offer will significantly impact your revenue. Residential cleaning typically involves regular home cleaning tasks and may generate steady revenue if you have recurring weekly or bi-weekly appointments. Commercial cleaning often involves larger spaces and could potentially generate higher revenue, but it might also require more resources. Specialized cleaning services like carpet cleaning or window cleaning often

command higher prices due to the specialized skills or equipment required.
2. **Pricing Strategy**: Your pricing strategy is another critical factor in your revenue model. You could charge an hourly rate, which gives clients flexibility, or a flat fee, which provides clients with predictability. Contract-based pricing, where you provide regular cleaning services over a specified period, can also provide a steady income stream.
3. **Additional Services**: Offering additional services like deep cleaning or green cleaning can also contribute to your revenue. These services often command higher prices and can attract clients who are willing to pay a premium for these specialized services.

Cost Structure

The cost structure refers to the various costs incurred in running your cleaning business. It includes both fixed costs (costs that do not change regardless of the volume of business activity) and variable costs (costs that change in proportion to the volume of business activity).

1. **Fixed Costs**: Fixed costs for a cleaning business might include costs such as business licenses and permits, insurance, rent or mortgage payments for your office space, utilities, and salaries for any administrative staff or salaried cleaning staff.
2. **Variable Costs**: Variable costs for a cleaning business typically include wages for hourly

cleaning staff, cleaning supplies and equipment, transportation costs, and marketing costs. These costs will increase as the volume of your business activity increases.

Financial Projections

Financial projections are forecasts of how your business will perform financially in the future. They include projected income statements, balance sheets, and cash flow statements. Financial projections help you anticipate future revenue and expenses, plan for growth, and manage cash flow. They are also crucial for securing funding or investment, as lenders and investors want to see that your business has the potential to be profitable.

1. **Projected Income Statement**: The projected income statement shows your expected revenue, costs, and profits over a specific period. It helps you anticipate your profitability and identify any potential financial issues.
2. **Projected Balance Sheet**: The projected balance sheet provides a snapshot of your business's financial position at a specific point in time. It shows your assets, liabilities, and equity, helping you understand your business's financial health.
3. **Projected Cash Flow Statement**: The projected cash flow statement shows how changes in the balance sheet and income statement will affect cash and cash equivalents. It helps you manage your cash

flow and ensure that you have enough cash to cover your expenses.

Financial planning is a critical aspect of developing your business plan. By carefully planning your revenue model, cost structure, and financial projections, you can set your cleaning business up for financial success. Remember, the numbers in your financial plan are not just figures; they tell the story of your business's financial health and viability. So, take the time to create a detailed and accurate financial plan. It will serve as a valuable tool for managing your business's finances and driving its growth.

Chapter 4: Legalities and Licenses

Legal compliance is a critical aspect of running any business, including a cleaning business. It involves understanding and adhering to the laws and regulations that govern your business operations. This not only ensures the legality and legitimacy of your business but also helps protect your business from legal risks and penalties.

The Importance of Legal Compliance

Legal compliance is not just about obeying the law; it's about protecting your business, your employees, and your customers. Here's why legal compliance is important:

1. **Ensures Legality and Legitimacy**: Complying with the law is the first step towards establishing a legal and legitimate business. It gives your business a legal identity and makes it a recognized entity under the law.
2. **Protects Your Business**: Legal compliance helps protect your business from legal risks and penalties. Non-compliance can result in fines, penalties, lawsuits, and even the closure of your business.
3. **Builds Trust and Reputation**: A business that complies with the law is likely to earn the trust of its customers, employees, and other stakeholders. It enhances your business's reputation and can give you a competitive edge.

4. **Promotes Fair Business Practices**: Legal compliance promotes fair business practices. It ensures that your business operates in a manner that is fair to its customers, employees, and competitors.

Understanding Legal Requirements

Understanding the legal requirements of running a cleaning business can be complex, as it involves various laws and regulations at the local, state, and federal levels. Here are some of the key legal aspects you need to consider:

1. **Business Registration**: You need to register your business with the appropriate government agency. The process and requirements for business registration vary depending on your business structure (sole proprietorship, partnership, corporation, etc.) and your location.
2. **Licenses and Permits**: Depending on your location and the nature of your cleaning services, you may need certain licenses and permits to operate your business. For example, you may need a business license, a health and safety permit, or a professional cleaning license.
3. **Insurance**: Insurance is crucial for protecting your business from potential liabilities. Depending on your business operations, you may need various types of insurance, such as general liability insurance, workers'

compensation insurance, and commercial auto insurance.
4. **Employment Laws**: If you have employees, you need to comply with various employment laws. These include laws related to minimum wage, overtime, workplace safety, workers' compensation, and anti-discrimination.
5. **Tax Laws**: As a business owner, you are responsible for paying various taxes, such as income tax, sales tax, and employment taxes. You need to understand your tax obligations and ensure timely and accurate tax reporting and payment.

Legal compliance is a critical aspect of running a cleaning business. It ensures the legality and legitimacy of your business, protects your business from legal risks, and enhances your business's reputation.

Legal Compliance

Starting a cleaning business, like any other business, involves several legal considerations. It's crucial to ensure that your business is legally compliant right from the start. This involves registering your business and obtaining the necessary licenses and permits. Let's delve into these aspects in detail.

Registering Your Business

Business registration is the first step towards establishing your cleaning business. It gives your business a legal identity and makes it a recognized entity under the law. Here's a step-by-step guide on how to register your business:

1. **Choose a Business Name**: The first step in registering your business is choosing a business name. This name should reflect your brand and be easy for your customers to remember. Make sure the name you choose is unique and not already in use by another business.
2. **Choose a Business Structure**: The next step is to decide on a business structure. This could be a sole proprietorship, partnership, limited liability company (LLC), or corporation. Each structure has its own advantages and disadvantages, and the choice depends on factors like the size of your business, the level of control you want to have, the financial risks you are willing to take, and your tax planning strategy.
3. **Register Your Business**: Once you've chosen a business name and structure, you can proceed to register your business. The process and requirements for business registration vary depending on your location and the type of business structure you've chosen. Generally, this involves filing certain documents and paying a registration fee.
4. **Obtain an Employer Identification Number (EIN)**: An EIN, also known as a Federal Tax Identification Number, is used to identify a business entity for tax purposes. You can apply for an EIN through the IRS website.

Obtaining Necessary Licenses and Permits

Once your business is registered, the next step is to obtain the necessary licenses and permits. The specific licenses and permits you need will depend on the nature of your cleaning services and your location. Here's a general guide on how to go about it:

1. **Identify Required Licenses and Permits**: Start by identifying the licenses and permits required for your cleaning business. This could include a general business license, a cleaning business license, or specialized permits for certain types of cleaning services. The requirements vary by location, so it's important to check with your local and state government agencies.
2. **Apply for Licenses and Permits**: Once you've identified the required licenses and permits, the next step is to apply for them. This typically involves filling out an application form, paying a fee, and in some cases, passing an examination or meeting certain qualifications.
3. **Stay Compliant**: Obtaining your licenses and permits is not a one-time task. Most licenses and permits need to be renewed periodically. Additionally, you must comply with any regulations associated with the licenses and permits, such as safety regulations or environmental regulations.

Registering your business and obtaining the necessary licenses and permits are crucial steps in starting your cleaning business. They ensure the legality and legitimacy of your business, protect your business from legal risks, and build trust with your customers.

Industry Regulations

Understanding industry regulations and ensuring compliance with them is a critical aspect of running a cleaning business. These regulations are designed to ensure the safety and health of both your employees and clients, protect the environment, and maintain a certain standard of service in the cleaning industry.

Understanding Industry Regulations

Industry regulations for the cleaning business can be broadly categorized into three areas: health and safety regulations, environmental regulations, and service standards.

1. **Health and Safety Regulations**: These regulations are designed to ensure the safety and health of your employees and clients. They cover areas such as the safe use of cleaning chemicals, proper handling and disposal of waste, provision of personal protective equipment (PPE) for employees, and adherence to safe work practices. For example, the Occupational Safety and Health Administration (OSHA) in the United States sets and enforces standards to ensure safe and healthy working conditions.
2. **Environmental Regulations**: These regulations aim to minimize the

environmental impact of cleaning activities. They typically cover the use and disposal of cleaning chemicals, waste management, and pollution control. For instance, you may be required to use environmentally friendly cleaning products, or follow specific procedures for disposing of cleaning waste.
3. **Service Standards**: These regulations are designed to ensure a certain standard of service in the cleaning industry. They may cover aspects such as the qualifications and training of cleaning staff, the quality of cleaning services, and customer service standards. Compliance with these standards can enhance your business's reputation and customer satisfaction.

How to Comply with Industry Regulations

Compliance with industry regulations is not just about understanding the regulations; it's about integrating them into your business operations. Here are some steps to ensure compliance:

1. **Stay Informed**: Regulations can change over time, so it's important to stay informed about the latest regulations applicable to your business. This can be done by regularly checking the websites of regulatory bodies, subscribing to industry newsletters, or joining industry associations.
2. **Implement Policies and Procedures**: Develop and implement policies and procedures that reflect the requirements of

the regulations. This could include safety procedures for using cleaning chemicals, waste disposal procedures, or customer service policies.
3. **Train Your Staff**: Ensure that your staff are aware of the regulations and understand how to comply with them. This could involve regular training sessions, providing written guidelines, or on-the-job coaching.
4. **Monitor Compliance**: Regularly monitor your business's compliance with the regulations. This could involve regular audits, inspections, or reviews of your policies and procedures.
5. **Take Corrective Action**: If you identify any areas of non-compliance, take immediate corrective action. This could involve revising your policies, retraining your staff, or making changes to your business operations.

Understanding industry regulations and ensuring compliance is a critical aspect of running a cleaning business. It not only ensures the legality and legitimacy of your business but also enhances your business's reputation, protects your business from legal risks, and contributes to the safety and satisfaction of your employees and clients.

Non-Compliance

Non-compliance with legal requirements and industry regulations can have serious consequences for your cleaning business. It can lead to penalties, damage your reputation, and even result in the closure of your business. In this section, we will discuss the consequences of non-compliance and provide guidance on how to avoid them.

Consequences of Non-Compliance

1. **Legal Penalties**: Non-compliance with laws and regulations can result in legal penalties. These can include fines, sanctions, or even criminal charges. For example, if you fail to comply with health and safety regulations, you could be fined or face legal action.
2. **Damage to Reputation**: Non-compliance can also damage your business's reputation. If customers, employees, or the public learn that your business is not complying with legal requirements, it could harm your business's image and lead to loss of customers or business opportunities.
3. **Loss of Business License**: In severe cases, non-compliance could lead to the revocation of your business license. This would result in the closure of your business.
4. **Increased Costs**: Non-compliance can also lead to increased costs. For example, you may need to pay fines or legal fees, or you may need to invest in changes to your business operations to achieve compliance.

How to Avoid Non-Compliance

Avoiding non-compliance involves understanding the legal requirements and industry regulations applicable to your business, implementing policies and procedures to ensure compliance, and regularly monitoring and reviewing your compliance.

1. **Understand Legal Requirements and Industry Regulations**: The first step in avoiding non-compliance is to understand the legal requirements and industry regulations applicable to your cleaning business. This involves researching laws and regulations, consulting with legal experts, and staying updated on changes in laws and regulations.
2. **Implement Policies and Procedures**: Once you understand the legal requirements, you should implement policies and procedures to ensure compliance. This could involve developing a compliance program, training your staff on compliance requirements, and establishing procedures for reporting and addressing non-compliance.
3. **Monitor and Review Compliance**: Regularly monitor and review your compliance with legal requirements. This could involve conducting internal audits, seeking feedback from staff, and reviewing your compliance program.
4. **Take Corrective Action**: If you identify any areas of non-compliance, take immediate corrective action. This could involve revising your policies, retraining your staff, or making changes to your business operations.

Compliance with legal requirements and industry regulations is crucial for the success and sustainability of your cleaning business. By understanding the consequences of non-compliance and taking proactive steps to ensure compliance, you can protect your business from legal risks, maintain a positive reputation, and ensure the longevity of your business.

Chapter 5: Equipment and Supplies

In the cleaning business, the role of equipment and supplies is paramount. They are the backbone of your operations, enabling you to deliver the cleaning services that your clients need. From brooms and mops to cleaning solutions and protective gear, the right equipment and supplies can make the difference between a job well done and a dissatisfied customer.

The Role of Equipment in a Cleaning Business

Equipment is the workhorse of your cleaning business. It's what enables you to clean efficiently and effectively. Here's why equipment is so important:

1. **Efficiency**: The right equipment can help you clean faster and more efficiently. For example, a high-quality vacuum cleaner can pick up more dirt in less time than a lower-quality model. This can help you complete cleaning jobs more quickly, allowing you to serve more clients and generate more revenue.
2. **Effectiveness**: The right equipment can also help you clean more effectively. For example, a steam cleaner can remove dirt and grime that a regular mop might leave behind. This can help you deliver a higher level of cleanliness, which can impress your clients and lead to repeat business.
3. **Professionalism**: Using professional-grade equipment can also enhance your image as a professional cleaning service. When clients see that you use high-quality, professional

equipment, they're likely to have more confidence in your ability to deliver top-notch cleaning services.

The Role of Supplies in a Cleaning Business

While equipment is crucial, it's only part of the equation. You also need the right cleaning supplies to do your job. Here's why supplies are so important:

1. **Effectiveness**: Just as with equipment, the right cleaning supplies can help you clean more effectively. High-quality cleaning solutions can remove stains, dirt, and bacteria that water alone can't handle. This can help you achieve a deeper clean and ensure your clients' satisfaction.
2. **Safety**: Some cleaning tasks require specific supplies for safety reasons. For example, you might need gloves to protect your hands from harsh cleaning chemicals, or masks to prevent the inhalation of dust or fumes. Using these supplies can help ensure your safety and the safety of your clients.
3. **Compliance**: In some cases, you might be legally required to use certain supplies. For example, if you're cleaning a restaurant kitchen, you might need to use cleaning solutions that are approved for use in food service areas. Using these supplies can help you comply with health and safety regulations.

Equipment and supplies play a critical role in a cleaning business. They enable you to clean efficiently and effectively, project a professional image, ensure safety, and comply with regulations. Choosing the right equipment and supplies for your cleaning business is therefore a decision that requires careful consideration.

Sourcing Equipment & Supplies

Sourcing equipment and supplies effectively is a critical aspect of running a successful cleaning business. The right equipment and supplies can help you deliver high-quality cleaning services, enhance your efficiency, and ensure the safety of your staff and clients. Here's a comprehensive guide on how to source equipment and supplies effectively:

Identify Your Needs

The first step in sourcing equipment and supplies is to identify your needs. What types of cleaning services will you offer? What equipment and supplies will you need to deliver these services? Your needs will depend on the nature of your cleaning services. For example, if you're offering residential cleaning services, you might need basic cleaning equipment like brooms, mops, vacuum cleaners, and cleaning solutions. If you're offering commercial cleaning services, you might need more specialized equipment like carpet cleaners or floor polishers.

Research Suppliers

Once you've identified your needs, the next step is to research suppliers. There are many suppliers of cleaning equipment and supplies, so it's important to choose the right one for your business. Consider factors like the range of products, prices, quality, reliability, and customer service. You can find suppliers through online searches, industry directories, trade shows, or recommendations from other businesses.

Compare Prices and Quality

When choosing a supplier, don't just consider the price. While it's important to find equipment and supplies that fit your budget, you also need to consider the quality. Cheap, low-quality equipment and supplies might save you money in the short term, but they could cost you more in the long term due to higher maintenance costs, shorter lifespan, or poor performance. Compare prices and quality from different suppliers to find the best value for your money.

Consider Buying vs. Leasing

For some types of equipment, you might have the option to buy or lease. Buying equipment means you own it and can use it for as long as it lasts, but it requires a significant upfront investment. Leasing equipment means you pay a monthly fee to use it, which can be more affordable in the short term, but could cost you more in the long term. Consider the pros and cons of buying vs. leasing to decide which option is best for your business.

Plan for Maintenance and Replacement

Cleaning equipment and supplies will wear out over time and will need to be maintained and eventually replaced. Plan for these costs in your budget and schedule regular maintenance to keep your equipment in good working condition. Also, keep track of the lifespan of your equipment and plan for replacement before it breaks down.

Stay Updated on New Products and Technologies

The cleaning industry is constantly evolving, with new products and technologies being introduced all the time. Stay updated on these developments and consider investing in new equipment or supplies that can improve your efficiency, effectiveness, or safety.

Sourcing equipment and supplies effectively is crucial for the success of your cleaning business. By identifying your needs, researching suppliers, comparing prices and quality, considering buying vs. leasing, planning for maintenance and replacement, and staying updated on new products and technologies, you can ensure that you have the right equipment and supplies to deliver high-quality cleaning services.

Managing Resources

Efficient management of resources is a key aspect of running a successful cleaning business. It involves ensuring that your equipment and supplies are used effectively and sustainably, minimizing waste, and maximizing productivity. Here's a comprehensive guide on how to manage your resources efficiently:

Inventory Management

Inventory management involves tracking your equipment and supplies, ensuring that you have enough stock to meet your needs, and avoiding overstocking or understocking.

1. **Track Your Inventory**: Keep a record of all your equipment and supplies. This includes what you have in stock, where it's located, and its condition. You can use inventory management software to automate this process.
2. **Forecast Your Needs**: Based on your past usage and future business projections, forecast your future needs for equipment and supplies. This can help you plan your purchases and avoid running out of stock or overstocking.
3. **Manage Your Purchases**: Plan your purchases based on your forecasted needs. Try to take advantage of bulk purchasing discounts, but avoid buying more than you need just to get a discount. Overstocking can lead to waste and tie up your capital.

Equipment Maintenance and Replacement

Proper maintenance and timely replacement of equipment can prolong its lifespan, improve its performance, and reduce repair costs.

1. **Regular Maintenance**: Regularly clean and maintain your equipment according to the manufacturer's instructions. This can prevent damage, improve efficiency, and extend the lifespan of the equipment.
2. **Timely Repairs**: If a piece of equipment is damaged or not working properly, repair it as soon as possible. Delaying repairs can lead to further damage and higher repair costs.
3. **Planned Replacement**: Plan for the replacement of your equipment before it breaks down. This can prevent disruptions to your business and give you time to find the best deal.

Sustainable Use of Supplies

Sustainable use of supplies involves using your cleaning supplies in a way that meets your needs while minimizing waste and environmental impact.

1. **Use Supplies Efficiently**: Train your staff to use cleaning supplies efficiently. This can reduce waste, save money, and lessen the environmental impact of your cleaning activities.
2. **Choose Eco-Friendly Supplies**: Consider using eco-friendly cleaning supplies. These products can reduce your environmental impact and can be a selling point for environmentally conscious clients.
3. **Recycle and Dispose of Waste Properly**: Recycle whenever possible and dispose of waste in accordance with local regulations.

Improper disposal of cleaning waste can harm the environment and result in fines.

Efficient management of resources is crucial for the success of your cleaning business. It can help you reduce costs, improve productivity, and lessen your environmental impact. By implementing effective inventory management practices, maintaining and replacing your equipment appropriately, and using your supplies sustainably, you can ensure that your resources are managed efficiently.

Importance of Quality

The use of high-quality equipment and supplies is a critical factor in the success of a cleaning business. It directly impacts the effectiveness of your cleaning services, the satisfaction of your clients, and the productivity and safety of your cleaning staff. In this section, we will delve into the importance of using high-quality equipment and supplies in your cleaning business.

Specific Equipment Needs

The specific equipment you need will depend on the type of cleaning services you offer. For residential cleaning services, basic equipment may include:

- Vacuum cleaners: A high-quality vacuum cleaner is essential for removing dust and dirt from carpets and upholstery. You may need several vacuum cleaners if you have multiple cleaning teams.

- Mops and buckets: These are necessary for cleaning hard floors. Consider investing in microfiber mops, which can clean more effectively than traditional cotton mops.
- Cleaning cloths: Microfiber cleaning cloths are effective for dusting and can be used wet or dry on various surfaces.
- Protective gear: This includes gloves, masks, and possibly protective eyewear, depending on the cleaning products used.

For commercial cleaning services, you may need additional equipment such as:

- Carpet cleaners: These are necessary for deep cleaning of carpets in office buildings and other commercial spaces.
- Floor polishers: These are used for cleaning and polishing hard floors in commercial spaces.
- Power washers: These can be used for exterior cleaning tasks, such as cleaning windows or building exteriors.

Quantities of Supplies and Associated Expenses

The quantities of cleaning supplies you need will depend on the volume of your cleaning jobs. As a starting point, you might need the following quantities per cleaning team per month:

- All-purpose cleaner: 5 gallons
- Toilet cleaner: 2 gallons
- Window cleaner: 2 gallons

- Cleaning cloths: 50-100 cloths
- Mop heads: 5-10 mop heads

The expenses associated with these supplies can vary widely depending on the brand, quality, and where you purchase them. For example, a gallon of all-purpose cleaner can cost anywhere from $10 to $30. A high-quality vacuum cleaner can cost several hundred dollars, while a mop bucket and wringer can cost around $50 to $100.

Resources for Sourcing Equipment and Supplies

There are many resources available for sourcing cleaning equipment and supplies. These include:

- Wholesale suppliers: These companies sell cleaning equipment and supplies in bulk, often at lower prices than retail stores.
- Online retailers: Many online retailers sell cleaning equipment and supplies. This can be a convenient option, as you can compare prices and read reviews from other customers.
- Local stores: Some local stores may sell cleaning equipment and supplies. This can be a good option if you need to buy supplies quickly or if you want to see the products in person before buying.

Creating a budget for equipment and supplies in your cleaning business involves several steps:
1. **Identify Your Needs**: The first step is to identify what equipment and supplies you need. This will depend on the type of cleaning

services you offer. For example, a residential cleaning service might need vacuum cleaners, mops, brooms, cleaning solutions, gloves, and more. A commercial cleaning service might need additional equipment like carpet cleaners or floor polishers.
2. **Research Costs**: Once you've identified your needs, research how much each item costs. You can do this by checking prices online, contacting suppliers, or visiting local stores. Be sure to consider both the initial purchase cost and ongoing costs such as maintenance and replacement.
3. **Estimate Usage**: Estimate how much of each supply you'll use in a given period (for example, per month or per year). This will depend on factors like how many jobs you do and how much of each supply is used per job. For equipment, consider the lifespan of the equipment to estimate when it will need to be replaced.
4. **Calculate Total Costs**: Multiply the cost of each item by the quantity you need to get the total cost. Do this for both equipment and supplies. Add these totals together to get the total cost for your equipment and supplies.
5. **Include in Your Overall Budget**: Include the total cost for equipment and supplies in your overall business budget. This should be part of your startup costs if you're just starting your business, or part of your operating costs if your business is already operational.
6. **Plan for Unexpected Costs**: It's a good idea to set aside some money for unexpected costs.

For example, a piece of equipment might break down and need to be replaced sooner than expected.

7. **Review and Adjust Regularly**: Your equipment and supplies budget isn't set in stone. You should review and adjust it regularly based on your actual usage and costs. This can help you manage your costs more effectively and keep your business profitable.

Remember, investing in high-quality equipment and supplies can pay off in the long run by enabling you to provide better service to your clients. So, while it's important to manage costs, it's also important to not compromise on the quality of your equipment and supplies.

Chapter 6: Hiring and Training Staff

Human resources play a pivotal role in the success of a cleaning business. The quality of your services is largely determined by the competence and dedication of your staff. Therefore, hiring the right people and investing in their training is crucial. In this section, we will delve into the importance of human resources in a cleaning business.

The Role of Human Resources

Human resources, in the context of a cleaning business, primarily refers to your cleaning staff. They are the ones who interact with your clients, carry out the cleaning tasks, and represent your business. Here's why human resources are so important:

1. **Service Delivery**: Your cleaning staff are responsible for delivering the cleaning services that your clients pay for. Their ability to clean effectively and efficiently directly impacts your clients' satisfaction and your business's reputation.
2. **Customer Interaction**: In many cases, your cleaning staff are the face of your business. They interact with your clients, respond to their queries, and address their concerns. Their professionalism, courtesy, and communication skills can greatly influence how your clients perceive your business.
3. **Business Representation**: Your cleaning staff represent your business. Their appearance, behavior, and work ethic reflect on your business. If they present themselves

well and do their job diligently, it enhances your business's image.

Hiring the Right Staff

Hiring the right staff is crucial for the success of your cleaning business. Here are some factors to consider when hiring:
1. **Skills and Experience**: Cleaning is a skill that requires training and experience. When hiring cleaning staff, look for individuals who have relevant cleaning experience or are willing to undergo training.
2. **Work Ethic**: Cleaning can be physically demanding and sometimes monotonous. It's important to hire individuals who have a strong work ethic, are reliable, and are willing to do the hard work.
3. **Character**: Since your cleaning staff will be entering your clients' homes or offices, it's crucial to hire individuals of good character. They should be trustworthy, respectful, and professional.

Investing in Training

Training is an investment in your human resources that can pay off in the form of higher quality services, fewer mistakes, and more satisfied clients. Here are some reasons why training is important:
1. **Skill Development**: Training helps your cleaning staff develop the skills they need to clean effectively and efficiently. This can include technical cleaning skills, safety practices, and customer service skills.

2. **Quality Improvement**: Through training, your cleaning staff can learn how to improve the quality of their work. This can lead to cleaner, healthier environments for your clients and fewer complaints.
3. **Professionalism**: Training can also instill a sense of professionalism in your cleaning staff. It can teach them how to present themselves, how to interact with clients, and how to handle challenging situations.

Human resources are a critical aspect of a cleaning business. Hiring the right staff and investing in their training can lead to higher quality services, more satisfied clients, and a better reputation for your business.

Hiring Strategies

Hiring the right people is a critical aspect of running a successful cleaning business. Your employees are the face of your business, interacting directly with your clients, and their performance can significantly impact your business's reputation and client satisfaction. In this section, we will delve into the process of hiring the right people for your cleaning business.

Understanding Your Needs

Before you start the hiring process, it's important to understand your needs. What roles do you need to fill? What skills and qualities are you looking for in your employees? For a cleaning business, you might need cleaners, supervisors, and possibly administrative staff. The skills and qualities you might look for could include experience with cleaning tasks, attention to detail, reliability, and good customer service skills.

Creating a Job Description

Once you understand your needs, the next step is to create a job description for each role. A good job description should include the title of the role, a summary of the role's main duties and responsibilities, the skills and qualifications required, and any physical requirements (for example, the ability to lift heavy equipment). The job description serves as a guide for what you're looking for in a candidate and provides potential applicants with a clear understanding of what the job entails.

Advertising the Job

There are many ways to advertise a job vacancy. You could post the job on online job boards, advertise in local newspapers, or use social media. You could also reach out to your network and ask for referrals. When advertising the job, be sure to include the job description and information on how to apply.

Screening Applicants

Once you start receiving applications, the next step is to screen the applicants. This involves reviewing resumes and cover letters, checking references, and conducting initial interviews. Look for candidates who meet the requirements outlined in the job description and show potential to be good employees.

Conducting Interviews

The interview process gives you a chance to further assess the suitability of the candidates. Prepare a list of questions that will help you evaluate the candidates' skills, experience, and fit for your business. For example, you might ask about their previous cleaning experience, how they handle difficult situations, or why they're interested in working for your business.

Making a Hiring Decision

After conducting interviews, you can make a hiring decision. Consider the candidates' qualifications, interview performance, and any other relevant factors. Once you've made a decision, notify the successful candidate and provide them with a job offer.

Onboarding New Employees

Once a new employee is hired, it's important to properly onboard them. This involves providing training on their job duties, your business policies, and any health and safety procedures. Proper onboarding can help new employees get up to speed quickly and start contributing to your business.

Hiring the right people is a critical aspect of running a successful cleaning business. By understanding your needs, creating clear job descriptions, effectively advertising your job vacancies, carefully screening applicants, conducting thorough interviews, making informed hiring decisions, and properly onboarding new employees, you can build a strong team that contributes to the success of your business.

Training

Training your staff effectively is a critical aspect of running a successful cleaning business. Well-trained staff can deliver high-quality cleaning services, work efficiently, and represent your business professionally. In this section, we will delve into the process of training your staff effectively.

Understanding Training Needs

The first step in training your staff effectively is to understand their training needs. This involves identifying the skills and knowledge they need to perform their jobs effectively. For a cleaning business, this might include technical cleaning skills, safety procedures, customer service skills, and knowledge of your business policies and procedures.

Developing a Training Program

Once you've identified your staff's training needs, the next step is to develop a training program that addresses these needs. A good training program should be comprehensive, practical, and engaging. Here are some elements to consider when developing your training program:

1. **Technical Cleaning Skills**: This is the core of your training program. Your staff need to know how to clean effectively and efficiently. This includes knowing how to use cleaning equipment, how to apply cleaning techniques, and how to use cleaning supplies safely and effectively.

2. **Safety Procedures**: Cleaning can involve certain risks, such as exposure to cleaning chemicals or physical strain from lifting heavy equipment. Your training program should include safety procedures to minimize these risks. This could involve training on how to handle cleaning chemicals safely, how to use equipment without straining oneself, and what to do in case of an accident.
3. **Customer Service Skills**: As your staff will be interacting with your clients, they need to have good customer service skills. This includes being polite and respectful, responding to clients' requests or complaints effectively, and representing your business professionally.
4. **Business Policies and Procedures**: Your staff need to understand your business policies and procedures. This includes your policies on things like punctuality, dress code, handling client property, and dealing with client complaints.

Delivering the Training

Once you've developed your training program, the next step is to deliver the training to your staff. There are several methods you can use to deliver training, including on-the-job training, classroom training, online training, or a combination of these. Choose a method that is effective and convenient for your staff.

Evaluating the Training

After the training has been delivered, it's important to evaluate its effectiveness. This can be done through observation, feedback from staff, feedback from clients, or formal assessments. If the training is not as effective as you'd like, consider revising your training program or trying different training methods.

Continuous Learning and Development

Training should not be a one-time event, but a continuous process of learning and development. Encourage your staff to continuously improve their skills and knowledge, provide them with opportunities for further training or development, and recognize and reward their efforts to improve.

Training your staff effectively is crucial for the success of your cleaning business. By understanding your staff's training needs, developing a comprehensive training program, delivering the training effectively, evaluating the training, and promoting continuous learning and development, you can ensure that your staff have the skills and knowledge they need to deliver high-quality cleaning services.

Employee Relations & Work Environment

Effective employee management and creating a positive work environment are crucial aspects of running a successful cleaning business. They can enhance employee satisfaction, improve productivity, and reduce staff turnover. In this section, we will delve into how to manage your staff effectively and create a positive work environment.

Effective Employee Management

Effective employee management involves leading, motivating, and supporting your employees to perform at their best. Here are some strategies for effective employee management:

1. **Clear Communication**: Clear and open communication is the foundation of effective employee management. Ensure that your employees understand their roles and responsibilities, your expectations, and the goals of your business. Regularly update them on any changes or developments in the business.
2. **Performance Feedback**: Regularly provide feedback on your employees' performance. Recognize and appreciate good performance, and provide constructive feedback on areas that need improvement. This can motivate your employees to improve their performance and contribute more to the business.
3. **Conflict Resolution**: Conflicts can arise in any workplace, and it's important to address them promptly and effectively. Encourage open and respectful communication, listen to all sides, and find a fair and satisfactory resolution.
4. **Career Development Opportunities**: Provide opportunities for your employees to learn and grow in their careers. This could involve training, mentoring, or opportunities to take on new responsibilities. This can

motivate your employees, improve their skills, and increase their loyalty to your business.

Creating a Positive Work Environment

A positive work environment can enhance employee satisfaction, improve productivity, and reduce staff turnover. Here are some strategies for creating a positive work environment:

1. **Respect and Fair Treatment**: Treat all your employees with respect and fairness. This includes respecting their rights, treating them fairly in terms of pay and working conditions, and not tolerating any form of discrimination or harassment.
2. **Positive Relationships**: Encourage positive relationships among your employees. This could involve team-building activities, social events, or simply encouraging a friendly and supportive atmosphere in the workplace.
3. **Work-Life Balance**: Recognize that your employees have lives outside of work, and support them in achieving a healthy work-life balance. This could involve flexible working hours, time off for personal matters, or support for stress management.
4. **Safety and Well-being**: Ensure that your workplace is safe and healthy. This involves complying with health and safety regulations, providing necessary safety equipment, and addressing any health and safety concerns promptly.

Effective employee management and a positive work environment are crucial for the success of your cleaning business. By leading, motivating, and supporting your employees, and by creating a workplace that is respectful, fair, supportive, and safe, you can enhance employee satisfaction, improve productivity, and build a successful cleaning business.

Chapter 7: Marketing and Customer Acquisition

Marketing plays a pivotal role in the success of a cleaning business. It's the vehicle through which you communicate your business's value proposition to potential customers, build your brand, and ultimately drive customer acquisition. In this section, we will delve into the role of marketing in a cleaning business.

Understanding the Importance of Marketing

Marketing is more than just advertising your services; it's about strategically positioning your business in the market, understanding your customers' needs, and finding effective ways to meet those needs. Here's why marketing is so important:

1. **Customer Acquisition**: The primary goal of marketing is to attract potential customers to your business. Effective marketing can help you reach a larger audience, generate leads, and convert those leads into customers.
2. **Brand Building**: Marketing also helps you build your brand. Your brand is what sets you apart from your competitors. It's what makes your business unique and memorable in the eyes of your customers.
3. **Customer Retention**: Good marketing isn't just about attracting new customers; it's also about keeping existing customers. By consistently delivering value and maintaining strong relationships with your customers, you

can foster loyalty and encourage repeat business.
4. **Business Growth**: Ultimately, effective marketing drives business growth. By attracting new customers and retaining existing ones, marketing can help you increase your revenue and grow your business.

Key Elements of a Marketing Strategy

A marketing strategy is a plan that outlines how you will achieve your marketing goals. Here are some key elements that you might include in your marketing strategy:

1. **Target Market**: Your target market is the group of customers that you aim to attract to your business. Understanding your target market is crucial for tailoring your marketing efforts to their needs and preferences.
2. **Value Proposition**: Your value proposition is the unique value that your business offers to customers. It's what sets you apart from your competitors. Your value proposition should be at the heart of all your marketing messages.
3. **Marketing Channels**: Marketing channels are the avenues through which you reach your target market. This could include traditional channels like print advertising or direct mail, digital channels like social media or email marketing, or personal selling.
4. **Marketing Mix**: The marketing mix refers to the combination of marketing tactics you use to promote your business. This typically

includes product (or service), price, place, and promotion – often referred to as the "4 Ps" of marketing.
5. **Budget**: Your marketing budget is the amount of money you allocate to your marketing activities. It's important to plan your budget carefully to ensure that you're investing your resources wisely.

Marketing plays a critical role in a cleaning business. By understanding the importance of marketing and developing a strategic marketing plan, you can attract and retain customers, build your brand, and drive business growth.

Traditional Marketing Methods

Traditional marketing methods, often referred to as outbound marketing, have been used by businesses for centuries to reach potential customers. Despite the rise of digital marketing, traditional marketing methods still hold value and can be highly effective when used strategically. In this section, we will delve into various traditional marketing methods and their effectiveness in a cleaning business.

Direct Mail

Direct mail involves sending promotional materials, such as flyers, brochures, or postcards, directly to potential customers through the mail. This method allows you to target specific geographic areas, which can be particularly useful for a cleaning business that operates in a specific locality.

Effectiveness: While direct mail may seem outdated in the digital age, it can still be highly effective. It offers a tangible and personal touch that digital marketing often lacks. However, the success of direct mail largely depends on the quality of your mailing list and the appeal of your promotional materials.

Print Advertising

Print advertising includes placing ads in newspapers, magazines, or other print media. This method allows you to reach a broad audience and can be particularly effective if your target customers are regular readers of the print media you choose.

Effectiveness: The effectiveness of print advertising has declined with the rise of digital media. However, it can still be effective for reaching certain demographics, particularly older adults who prefer print media over digital media.

Telemarketing

Telemarketing involves contacting potential customers directly by phone to promote your services. This method allows you to reach a large number of people quickly and to have a direct conversation with potential customers.

Effectiveness: Telemarketing can be effective, but it also has its challenges. Many people find telemarketing calls intrusive and annoying, and there are strict regulations governing telemarketing practices.

Networking and Word-of-Mouth

Networking involves building relationships with other business owners, community members, and potential customers. Word-of-mouth marketing involves encouraging your satisfied customers to recommend your services to others.

Effectiveness: Networking and word-of-mouth marketing can be highly effective. People are more likely to trust recommendations from people they know and respect. Plus, these methods are often cost-effective, as they rely on personal relationships rather than paid advertising.

Outdoor Advertising

Outdoor advertising includes methods like billboards, signage, and vehicle wraps. This method allows you to reach a broad audience, particularly in the local area where your outdoor advertising is displayed.

Effectiveness: Outdoor advertising can be effective for increasing brand awareness. However, it's often more difficult to measure its effectiveness compared to digital marketing methods.

While traditional marketing methods face increasing competition from digital marketing, they still hold value and can be highly effective when used strategically. The key is to understand your target customers and to choose the marketing methods that will reach them most effectively.

Digital Marketing Strategies

In the digital age, online marketing strategies have become an essential part of promoting a business. For a cleaning business, leveraging digital marketing can help you reach a wider audience, engage with potential customers, and build your brand online. In this section, we will delve into various digital marketing strategies and how to use them effectively.

Website

Your website serves as the digital storefront of your cleaning business. It's where potential customers can learn about your services, read testimonials, and get in touch with you.

1. **Design**: A well-designed website can create a strong first impression. Ensure your website is clean, easy to navigate, and reflects your brand's image.
2. **Content**: The content on your website should clearly communicate what your business offers. Include details about your cleaning services, pricing, and the areas you serve.
3. **SEO**: Search Engine Optimization (SEO) involves optimizing your website to rank higher in search engine results, making it easier for potential customers to find you.

Social Media

Social media platforms like Facebook, Instagram, and LinkedIn can be powerful marketing tools.

1. **Presence**: Establish a presence on platforms where your potential customers are likely to be. Regularly post updates, share photos of your work, and engage with your followers.
2. **Advertising**: Social media platforms offer targeted advertising options that can help you reach potential customers in your area.
3. **Reviews and Recommendations**: Encourage satisfied customers to leave reviews or recommend your services on social media.

Email Marketing

Email marketing involves sending promotional emails to people who have expressed interest in your services.

1. **Newsletter**: Send a regular newsletter with updates, special offers, or cleaning tips.
2. **Promotions**: Email is a great way to let customers know about special promotions or discounts.
3. **Personalization**: Personalize your emails to make customers feel valued and engaged.

Online Directories

Listing your business in online directories can help improve your visibility online.

1. **Google My Business**: A Google My Business listing can help your business appear in local search results and Google Maps.

2. **Yelp**: Yelp is a popular platform where people look for reviews of local businesses.
3. **Industry-Specific Directories**: Consider also listing your business in directories specific to the cleaning industry.

Paid Online Advertising

Paid online advertising, like Google Ads or social media ads, can help you reach a wider audience.

1. **Targeting**: These platforms allow you to target your ads based on location, demographics, and even the interests of the audience.
2. **Cost-Effectiveness**: You can set a budget that suits your business, and you only pay when someone clicks on your ad (pay-per-click advertising).
3. **Measurability**: Online ads provide detailed analytics so you can see how your ad is performing and adjust your strategy accordingly.

Digital marketing strategies offer numerous opportunities to promote your cleaning business, reach potential customers, and grow your business. By leveraging these strategies effectively, you can build a strong online presence, attract more customers, and stay ahead of the competition.

Customer Acquisition & Retention

Customer acquisition and retention are two key aspects of running a successful cleaning business. While customer acquisition focuses on attracting new customers, customer retention is about keeping existing customers and encouraging them to continue using your services. In this section, we will delve into strategies for both customer acquisition and retention.

Customer Acquisition Strategies

Customer acquisition is about attracting new customers to your business. Here are some strategies that can help you acquire new customers:

1. **Targeted Marketing**: Use targeted marketing strategies to reach potential customers who are likely to be interested in your cleaning services. This could involve online advertising targeted at people in your local area, or direct mail sent to homes or businesses in your area.
2. **Promotions and Discounts**: Offering promotions and discounts can be an effective way to attract new customers. For example, you could offer a discount for first-time customers, or a special package deal for new clients.
3. **Referral Programs**: Encourage your existing customers to refer their friends and family to your business. You could offer them a discount or other incentive for each successful referral.
4. **Partnerships**: Partner with other local businesses that offer complementary services. For example, a real estate agency might

recommend your cleaning services to their clients who are moving into a new home.

Customer Retention Strategies

Once you've acquired new customers, the next step is to keep them. Here are some strategies for customer retention:

1. **Quality Service**: The most important factor in customer retention is the quality of your service. Ensure that your cleaning services meet or exceed your customers' expectations.
2. **Customer Service**: Provide excellent customer service. Respond promptly and professionally to customer inquiries and complaints, and go the extra mile to make your customers happy.
3. **Loyalty Programs**: Implement a loyalty program that rewards your customers for sticking with your services. This could involve discounts, freebies, or other perks for customers who use your services regularly.
4. **Regular Communication**: Keep in touch with your customers through regular communication. This could involve sending them email newsletters, updating them on new services or promotions, or simply checking in with them to ensure they're satisfied with your service.

Customer acquisition and retention are crucial for the success of your cleaning business. By using targeted marketing strategies, offering promotions and discounts, implementing referral programs, and forming partnerships, you can attract new customers. And by providing quality service, excellent customer service, loyalty programs, and regular communication, you can keep your existing customers.

Chapter 8: Pricing and Contracts

Pricing your services competitively is a critical aspect of running a successful cleaning business. It's a delicate balance - price your services too high, and you might drive away potential customers; price them too low, and you might not make enough profit to sustain your business. In this section, we will delve into the importance of pricing your services competitively and provide some guidance on how to do so.

Understanding the Importance of Competitive Pricing

Competitive pricing is about setting the price of your services at a level that is attractive to customers while still allowing you to make a profit. Here's why competitive pricing is important:

1. **Attracting Customers**: Price is one of the main factors that customers consider when choosing a cleaning service. If your prices are competitive, you're more likely to attract customers.
2. **Maximizing Profits**: While it's important to attract customers, it's also important to make a profit. By pricing your services competitively, you can strike a balance between attracting customers and making a profit.
3. **Positioning Your Business**: Your prices can also help position your business in the market. For example, if you offer high-end cleaning

services, you might charge higher prices to reflect the quality of your services.

Factors to Consider When Pricing Your Services

When pricing your services, there are several factors to consider:
1. **Costs**: First and foremost, you need to cover your costs. This includes direct costs like cleaning supplies and labor, as well as indirect costs like marketing, administration, and overheads.
2. **Competition**: Look at what your competitors are charging for similar services. This can give you a benchmark for setting your prices.
3. **Value**: Consider the value that your services provide to your customers. If your services save your customers time, or if you offer superior quality or convenience, you might be able to charge higher prices.
4. **Target Market**: Consider the budget and preferences of your target market. If your target market is budget-conscious, you might need to price your services lower. If your target market values quality and is willing to pay for it, you might be able to charge higher prices.

Strategies for Competitive Pricing

Here are some strategies for pricing your services competitively:
1. **Cost-Plus Pricing**: This involves adding a markup to your costs to determine your price. The markup should be enough to cover your overheads and provide a profit.

2. **Market-Oriented Pricing**: This involves setting your prices based on what the market is willing to pay. This requires a good understanding of your market and your competition.
3. **Value-Based Pricing**: This involves setting your prices based on the value that your services provide to your customers. This requires a good understanding of your customers and the benefits that your services provide to them.

Pricing your services competitively is crucial for the success of your cleaning business. By understanding the importance of competitive pricing, considering key factors when pricing your services, and using effective pricing strategies, you can attract customers, maximize profits, and position your business effectively in the market.

Pricing Strategies

Choosing the right pricing strategy is a critical decision for your cleaning business. The price you charge for your services not only affects your profitability but also how your business is perceived by potential customers. In this section, we will delve into different pricing strategies and provide guidance on how to choose the right one for your cleaning business.

Cost-Plus Pricing

Cost-plus pricing is one of the simplest pricing strategies. It involves calculating the total cost of providing your service and then adding a markup to determine the price. The markup should be enough to cover your overheads and provide a profit.

Pros: This strategy ensures that all costs are covered and a profit is made on each job. It's straightforward and easy to calculate.

Cons: It doesn't take into account what customers are willing to pay or what competitors are charging. If your costs are higher than average, you could end up pricing yourself out of the market.

Competitive Pricing

Competitive pricing involves setting your prices based on what your competitors are charging. This requires researching your competitors' prices and then deciding whether to match, beat, or go above their prices.

Pros: This strategy ensures that your prices are in line with market expectations. It can be effective in markets where services are similar and price is a major factor in customers' decision-making.

Cons: It can lead to price wars, which can erode profits. It also doesn't take into account your own costs and value proposition.

Value-Based Pricing

Value-based pricing involves setting your prices based on the perceived value of your services to your customers. This requires understanding your customers' needs and how much they value your services.

Pros: This strategy allows you to charge higher prices if your customers perceive a high value in your services. It aligns your prices with your value proposition.

Cons: It can be difficult to accurately assess the perceived value of your services. It requires a deep understanding of your customers and may involve more complex pricing structures.

Penetration Pricing

Penetration pricing involves setting your prices low to attract customers and gain market share. Once you've established a customer base, you can gradually increase your prices.

Pros: This strategy can be effective for new businesses looking to attract customers quickly. It can help you establish a presence in the market.

Cons: It can lead to low initial profits and may attract price-sensitive customers who will leave when prices increase. It also risks undervaluing your services.

Choosing the Right Pricing Strategy

Choosing the right pricing strategy for your cleaning business depends on several factors:
1. **Cost Structure**: Understand your cost structure. This includes direct costs like labor and materials, and indirect costs like overheads.
2. **Customer Sensitivity to Price**: Understand your customers' sensitivity to price. If your

customers are price-sensitive, competitive or penetration pricing may be more effective. If they value quality and are willing to pay for it, value-based pricing may be more appropriate.
3. **Competitive Landscape**: Understand your competitive landscape. If the market is highly competitive with similar services, competitive pricing may be necessary. If your services are unique, value-based pricing may be more effective.
4. **Brand Positioning**: Consider your brand positioning. If you want to position your business as a high-quality, premium service, a higher price point may be justified.

Choosing the right pricing strategy is crucial for the success of your cleaning business. By understanding different pricing strategies and considering your cost structure, customer sensitivity to price, competitive landscape, and brand positioning, you can choose a pricing strategy that maximizes your profitability and aligns with your business goals.

Managing Contracts Effectively

Managing contracts effectively is a crucial aspect of running a successful cleaning business. Contracts are legal agreements between your business and your clients that outline the terms of your service, including what services will be provided, when and how they will be provided, and how much will be paid for them. In this section, we will delve into how to manage contracts effectively.

Understanding the Importance of Contracts

Contracts are important for several reasons:
1. **Clarity**: Contracts provide clarity by clearly outlining the expectations of both parties. This can help prevent misunderstandings and disputes.
2. **Protection**: Contracts provide legal protection for both parties. If one party fails to fulfill their obligations, the other party can use the contract to seek legal recourse.
3. **Professionalism**: Having a formal contract demonstrates professionalism. It shows that you take your business seriously and that you're committed to providing reliable, high-quality service.

Creating Effective Contracts

Creating an effective contract involves several key elements:
1. **Scope of Services**: Clearly define what services you will provide. This could include the type of cleaning services, the areas to be cleaned, and any additional services.
2. **Payment Terms**: Specify how much the client will pay for your services, when payment is due, and what payment methods are accepted.
3. **Duration and Termination**: Specify the duration of the contract and the conditions under which the contract can be terminated.
4. **Dispute Resolution**: Include a clause outlining how disputes will be resolved. This

could involve negotiation, mediation, or legal action.
5. **Liability and Insurance**: Include clauses that limit your liability and specify that you have appropriate insurance coverage.

Managing Contracts

Once a contract is in place, it needs to be managed effectively:

1. **Fulfill Your Obligations**: Ensure that you fulfill all your obligations as outlined in the contract. This includes providing the services as agreed, invoicing accurately and on time, and addressing any issues or concerns promptly.
2. **Monitor Contract Performance**: Regularly review the contract to ensure that it's working as intended. This could involve checking that services are being delivered as agreed, that payments are being made on time, and that both parties are satisfied with the arrangement.
3. **Renegotiate as Needed**: If circumstances change, or if the contract isn't working as well as expected, it may be necessary to renegotiate the contract. This should be done in a fair and transparent manner, with the aim of achieving a win-win outcome.
4. **Maintain Good Relationships**: Maintaining good relationships with your clients can help ensure that contracts are fulfilled smoothly. This involves communicating effectively,

treating clients with respect, and striving to exceed their expectations.

Managing contracts effectively is crucial for the success of your cleaning business. By understanding the importance of contracts, creating effective contracts, and managing them effectively, you can build strong, mutually beneficial relationships with your clients, protect your business interests, and enhance your business's reputation for professionalism and reliability.

Importance of Clear & Fair Contracts

Clear and fair contracts are the backbone of any successful business relationship, including those in the cleaning industry. They define the expectations of both parties, outline the scope of work, and provide a roadmap for resolving potential disputes. In this section, we will delve into the importance of clear and fair contracts and provide guidance on how to create them.

Understanding the Importance of Clear Contracts

A clear contract leaves no room for ambiguity. It outlines in detail the services to be provided, the responsibilities of each party, the payment terms, and the procedures for dispute resolution. Here's why clear contracts are important:

1. **Setting Expectations**: A clear contract sets the expectations for both parties. It outlines

what services will be provided, when and how they will be delivered, and how much will be paid for them.
2. **Preventing Misunderstandings**: By clearly stating the terms and conditions of the service, a clear contract can help prevent misunderstandings that could lead to disputes.
3. **Providing a Legal Framework**: A contract is a legally binding document. If one party fails to fulfill their obligations, the other party can use the contract to seek legal recourse.

The Importance of Fair Contracts

A fair contract is one that is balanced and considers the interests of both parties. It does not unduly favor one party over the other. Here's why fair contracts are important:

1. **Building Trust**: A fair contract can help build trust between you and your clients. It shows that you value your clients and are willing to treat them fairly.
2. **Encouraging Long-Term Relationships**: Clients are more likely to continue using your services if they feel that they are being treated fairly. A fair contract can encourage long-term business relationships.
3. **Enhancing Your Reputation**: Fair contracts not only benefit your clients, but they also enhance your business's reputation. They show that your business operates with integrity and respects its clients.

Creating Clear and Fair Contracts

Creating clear and fair contracts involves several key steps:

1. **Define the Scope of Services**: Clearly define what services you will provide. Be as specific as possible to avoid ambiguity.
2. **Outline Responsibilities**: Outline the responsibilities of both parties. This includes your responsibilities in delivering the service and the client's responsibilities, such as making timely payments.
3. **Specify Payment Terms**: Clearly specify the payment terms, including the amount, payment schedule, and acceptable payment methods.
4. **Include a Dispute Resolution Clause**: Include a clause that outlines how disputes will be resolved. This could involve negotiation, mediation, or legal action.
5. **Review and Revise**: Regularly review and revise your contracts to ensure they remain clear, fair, and relevant. This is particularly important as your business grows and evolves.

Clear and fair contracts are crucial for the success of your cleaning business. They set expectations, prevent misunderstandings, provide a legal framework, build trust, encourage long-term relationships, and enhance your reputation. By understanding the importance of clear and fair contracts and following the steps to create them, you can establish strong and successful business relationships with your clients.

Chapter 9: Customer Service and Retention

Customer service plays a pivotal role in the success of a cleaning business. It's the cornerstone of your relationship with your clients, and it can significantly impact your business's reputation, customer satisfaction, and customer retention. In this section, we will delve into the role of customer service in a cleaning business.

Understanding the Importance of Customer Service

Customer service is about meeting and exceeding your customers' expectations. It involves providing high-quality services, responding to customer inquiries and complaints promptly and professionally, and going the extra mile to ensure customer satisfaction. Here's why customer service is so important:

1. **Customer Satisfaction**: Good customer service leads to satisfied customers. Satisfied customers are more likely to continue using your services and recommend your business to others.
2. **Business Reputation**: Your business's reputation is largely shaped by the quality of your customer service. Good customer service can enhance your business's reputation, while poor customer service can harm it.
3. **Customer Retention**: Good customer service can help you retain customers. It's

often more cost-effective to retain existing customers than to acquire new ones, so customer retention is crucial for your business's profitability.
4. **Competitive Advantage**: Good customer service can give you a competitive advantage. In a competitive market, offering superior customer service can set your business apart from your competitors.

Key Elements of Good Customer Service

Good customer service involves several key elements:

1. **Quality Services**: The foundation of good customer service is providing high-quality cleaning services. This involves cleaning effectively and efficiently, paying attention to detail, and tailoring your services to meet your customers' needs.
2. **Prompt and Professional Responses**: Respond to customer inquiries and complaints promptly and professionally. Show empathy, provide clear and accurate information, and strive to resolve any issues to the customer's satisfaction.
3. **Reliability**: Be reliable. Show up on time, complete the cleaning as scheduled, and fulfill all your commitments to your customers.
4. **Going the Extra Mile**: Go the extra mile to exceed your customers' expectations. This could involve doing little extras during your

cleaning, being flexible to accommodate your customers' schedules, or simply showing that you care about your customers.

Improving Your Customer Service

Improving your customer service involves continuously assessing your current level of customer service and looking for ways to improve. Here are some strategies for improving your customer service:

1. **Customer Feedback**: Regularly seek feedback from your customers. This can help you understand what you're doing well and where you need to improve.
2. **Training**: Provide customer service training for your staff. This can help them develop the skills and knowledge they need to provide excellent customer service.
3. **Policies and Procedures**: Develop clear policies and procedures for handling customer inquiries and complaints. This can help ensure that all customer interactions are handled consistently and professionally.
4. **Continuous Improvement**: Strive for continuous improvement. Regularly review your customer service performance and look for ways to improve.

Customer service plays a critical role in a cleaning business. By understanding the importance of customer service, implementing the key elements of good customer service, and continuously striving to improve, you can enhance customer satisfaction, improve your business's reputation, retain customers, and gain a competitive advantage.

Handling Customer Complaints

Handling customer complaints effectively is a crucial aspect of customer service in a cleaning business. Complaints, when addressed properly, provide an opportunity to improve your services and strengthen your relationship with your customers. In this section, we will delve into how to handle customer complaints effectively.

Understanding the Importance of Handling Complaints Effectively

Customer complaints are inevitable in any business. However, the way you handle these complaints can significantly impact your business's reputation and your relationship with your customers. Here's why handling complaints effectively is important:

1. **Customer Satisfaction**: Resolving complaints to the customer's satisfaction can turn a negative experience into a positive one. It shows that you value your customers and are committed to providing high-quality service.
2. **Business Improvement**: Complaints can provide valuable feedback on your services. They can highlight areas where you need to improve, helping you to continually enhance your service quality.

3. **Reputation Management**: How you handle complaints can affect your business's reputation. Handling complaints effectively can enhance your reputation, while handling them poorly can harm it.

Strategies for Handling Complaints Effectively

Here are some strategies for handling customer complaints effectively:

1. **Listen and Understand**: The first step in handling a complaint is to listen to the customer's concerns and understand the problem. Show empathy and patience, and avoid getting defensive.
2. **Apologize and Acknowledge**: If your business is at fault, apologize sincerely to the customer. Even if the problem was not your fault, acknowledge the customer's feelings and the inconvenience caused.
3. **Find a Solution**: Work with the customer to find a solution to the problem. This could involve correcting the issue, offering a discount or refund, or providing an alternative service.
4. **Follow Up**: After resolving the complaint, follow up with the customer to ensure they are satisfied with the solution. This shows that you care about their satisfaction even after the complaint has been resolved.
5. **Learn and Improve**: Use the complaint as a learning opportunity. Analyze the issue, identify what went wrong, and make necessary

improvements to prevent similar complaints in the future.

Creating a Complaint Handling Process

Having a clear process for handling complaints can help ensure that all complaints are handled effectively and consistently. Here are some steps to create a complaint handling process:

1. **Establish Channels for Complaints**: Provide clear channels for customers to voice their complaints. This could include a phone number, email address, or social media channels.
2. **Train Your Staff**: Train your staff on how to handle complaints effectively. They should know how to listen and respond empathetically, how to resolve issues, and when to escalate complaints.
3. **Monitor and Review Complaints**: Regularly monitor and review complaints to identify common issues and trends. This can help you identify areas for improvement in your services.

Handling customer complaints effectively is crucial for the success of your cleaning business. By understanding the importance of handling complaints, implementing effective complaint handling strategies, and creating a clear complaint handling process, you can enhance customer satisfaction, improve your services, and manage your reputation effectively.

Improving Customer Satisfaction

Customer satisfaction is the cornerstone of a successful cleaning business. Satisfied customers are more likely to continue using your services, recommend your business to others, and contribute positively to your business's reputation. In this section, we will delve into various strategies to improve customer satisfaction in your cleaning business.

Understanding Customer Satisfaction

Customer satisfaction is a measure of how well your services meet or exceed your customers' expectations. High levels of customer satisfaction can lead to customer loyalty, positive word-of-mouth, and increased business growth. Conversely, low levels of customer satisfaction can lead to customer churn, negative reviews, and damage to your business's reputation.

Key Factors Influencing Customer Satisfaction

Several key factors can influence customer satisfaction in a cleaning business:

1. **Quality of Service**: The quality of your cleaning services is likely to be the most significant factor influencing customer satisfaction. This includes the thoroughness of the cleaning, attention to detail, and the overall result.

2. **Reliability**: Customers expect you to deliver your services reliably and on time. This includes arriving for scheduled appointments on time and completing the cleaning within the agreed timeframe.
3. **Professionalism**: The professionalism of your staff can also significantly impact customer satisfaction. This includes their appearance, behavior, and the way they interact with customers.
4. **Value for Money**: Customers also consider whether your services offer good value for money. This involves comparing the quality of your services with the price they pay.

Strategies to Improve Customer Satisfaction

Here are some strategies that can help you improve customer satisfaction:

1. **Improve Service Quality**: Continually strive to improve the quality of your cleaning services. This could involve investing in better cleaning equipment, implementing more effective cleaning techniques, or providing additional training for your staff.
2. **Enhance Reliability**: Ensure that you deliver your services reliably and on time. If delays or changes are unavoidable, communicate with your customers as early as possible and apologize for any inconvenience.
3. **Train Your Staff**: Provide customer service training for your staff to enhance their professionalism. This can help them interact

more effectively with customers, handle complaints more efficiently, and represent your business more positively.
4. **Offer Competitive Pricing**: Ensure that your prices are competitive and offer good value for money. Regularly review your pricing strategy and consider offering discounts or special offers to loyal customers.
5. **Solicit Customer Feedback**: Regularly solicit feedback from your customers to understand their needs and expectations better. Use this feedback to identify areas for improvement and implement necessary changes.
6. **Handle Complaints Effectively**: Handle customer complaints promptly and effectively. Apologize for any mistakes, correct the issue as quickly as possible, and take steps to prevent similar problems in the future.

Improving customer satisfaction should be a key goal for your cleaning business. By understanding the factors that influence customer satisfaction and implementing strategies to improve these areas, you can enhance customer loyalty, generate positive word-of-mouth, and drive business growth.

Customer Loyalty & Retention

Building customer loyalty and retaining customers are vital for the long-term success of a cleaning business. Loyal customers not only bring in steady revenue but can also become advocates for your business, recommending your services to others. In this section, we will delve into strategies for building customer loyalty and retaining customers.

Understanding Customer Loyalty

Customer loyalty is when customers choose your business over others, not just once, but repeatedly. Loyal customers are those who are satisfied with your service, trust your business, and therefore, choose to continue using your services. Here's why customer loyalty is important:

1. **Repeat Business**: Loyal customers provide repeat business, which can be more profitable than constantly acquiring new customers.
2. **Word-of-Mouth Marketing**: Loyal customers are likely to recommend your services to others, providing valuable word-of-mouth marketing.
3. **Feedback and Improvement**: Loyal customers can provide valuable feedback, helping you improve your services.

Strategies for Building Customer Loyalty

Here are some strategies to build customer loyalty:

1. **Provide Excellent Service**: The quality of your service is the foundation of customer loyalty. Ensure that your cleaning services meet or exceed your customers' expectations.
2. **Excellent Customer Service**: Provide excellent customer service. Respond promptly and professionally to customer inquiries and

complaints, and go the extra mile to make your customers happy.
3. **Loyalty Programs**: Implement a loyalty program that rewards your customers for sticking with your services. This could involve discounts, freebies, or other perks for customers who use your services regularly.
4. **Regular Communication**: Keep in touch with your customers through regular communication. This could involve sending them email newsletters, updating them on new services or promotions, or simply checking in with them to ensure they're satisfied with your service.

Customer Retention Strategies

While building customer loyalty is about encouraging customers to choose your services repeatedly, customer retention is about keeping customers over the long term. Here are some strategies for customer retention:

1. **Quality and Consistency**: Ensure that the quality of your service is consistently high. Customers are likely to stick with a service that they know they can rely on.
2. **Understand Your Customers**: Understand your customers' needs and expectations. This can help you tailor your services to meet their needs, increasing their satisfaction and likelihood to stay.
3. **Customer Engagement**: Engage with your customers regularly. This can involve regular

communication, asking for feedback, or offering special deals or promotions.
4. **Handle Complaints Effectively**: Handle customer complaints promptly and effectively. If customers see that you take their complaints seriously and are willing to resolve issues, they are more likely to stay.

Building customer loyalty and retaining customers are crucial for the success of your cleaning business. By providing excellent service, engaging with your customers, understanding their needs, and handling complaints effectively, you can build customer loyalty and retain customers over the long term.

Chapter 10: Growth and Expansion

Growth and expansion are vital aspects of a successful cleaning business. They involve increasing your customer base, expanding your service offerings, or extending your geographic reach. In this section, we will delve into the importance of growth and expansion for a cleaning business.

Understanding the Importance of Growth and Expansion

Growth and expansion are important for several reasons:

1. **Increased Revenue**: The most obvious benefit of growth and expansion is increased revenue. By attracting more customers, offering more services, or expanding into new areas, you can increase your income and profitability.
2. **Economies of Scale**: As your business grows, you can achieve economies of scale. This means that as you increase the volume of your services, the cost per unit of service can decrease, leading to higher profit margins.
3. **Brand Recognition**: Growth and expansion can also lead to increased brand recognition. As more people use your services and you become more visible in the market, your brand can become more recognized and trusted.
4. **Competitive Advantage**: A larger, more established business can have a competitive

advantage over smaller, newer businesses. You may have more resources, a larger customer base, and more experience, all of which can give you an edge over your competitors.

Strategies for Growth and Expansion

There are several strategies you can use to grow and expand your cleaning business:

1. **Marketing and Advertising**: Effective marketing and advertising can attract more customers to your business. This could involve traditional methods like print advertising or direct mail, or digital methods like social media marketing or search engine optimization.
2. **Diversification**: Diversification involves adding new services to your business. For example, if you currently offer residential cleaning services, you could diversify by offering commercial cleaning services or specialized cleaning services like carpet cleaning or window cleaning.
3. **Geographic Expansion**: Geographic expansion involves extending your services to new areas. This could involve opening new locations, franchising your business, or simply marketing your services to customers in new areas.
4. **Partnerships and Alliances**: Forming partnerships or alliances with other businesses can also facilitate growth and expansion. For

example, you could partner with a property management company to provide cleaning services for their properties.

Managing Growth and Expansion

While growth and expansion are beneficial, they also come with challenges. It's important to manage growth and expansion carefully to ensure that your business continues to operate efficiently and effectively. Here are some things to consider:

1. **Capacity**: Ensure that you have the capacity to handle increased demand. This could involve hiring more staff, investing in more equipment, or improving your business processes.
2. **Quality Control**: As your business grows, maintaining the quality of your services can become more challenging. Implement quality control measures to ensure that your services continue to meet high standards.
3. **Financial Management**: Growth and expansion often involve significant financial investment. Carefully plan and manage your finances to ensure that your growth and expansion plans are financially viable.

Growth and expansion are crucial for the success of your cleaning business. By understanding the importance of growth and expansion, implementing effective growth strategies, and managing growth carefully, you can increase your revenue, enhance your brand recognition, gain a competitive advantage, and drive your business's success.

Strategies for Scaling Operations

Scaling operations is a critical aspect of growth and expansion for a cleaning business. It involves increasing your capacity to deliver your services to a larger customer base or over a wider geographic area, without compromising the quality of your service. In this section, we will delve into strategies for scaling operations effectively.

Understanding the Importance of Scaling Operations

Scaling operations is important for several reasons:

1. **Meeting Increased Demand**: As your business grows, demand for your services is likely to increase. Scaling operations allows you to meet this increased demand effectively.
2. **Maintaining Service Quality**: As you serve more customers or expand to new areas, maintaining the quality of your service can become more challenging. Effective scaling ensures that service quality remains high, even as your business grows.
3. **Increasing Efficiency**: Scaling operations often involves improving efficiency. This could involve streamlining your processes, adopting new technologies, or optimizing resource allocation.

Strategies for Scaling Operations

Here are some strategies for scaling operations in a cleaning business:

1. **Hiring and Training Staff**: As your business grows, you'll likely need to hire more staff. It's important to have effective hiring and training processes in place to ensure that your new staff members are capable and well-prepared.
2. **Investing in Equipment and Supplies**: You may need to invest in more or better cleaning equipment and supplies to handle increased demand. Consider the cost, durability, and efficiency of the equipment and supplies you choose.
3. **Streamlining Processes**: Look for ways to streamline your cleaning and administrative processes. This could involve adopting new technologies, eliminating unnecessary steps, or reorganizing your workflow.
4. **Expanding Geographically**: If you're planning to expand geographically, consider the logistics carefully. This could involve opening new locations, hiring local staff, or investing in transportation.
5. **Building Partnerships**: Building partnerships with other businesses or contractors can also help you scale operations. For example, you could partner with a local laundry service to handle linens, freeing up your staff to focus on cleaning.

Managing the Challenges of Scaling Operations

Scaling operations can bring challenges, such as maintaining service quality, managing increased costs, and coordinating a larger workforce. Here are some tips for managing these challenges:

1. **Quality Control**: Implement quality control measures to ensure that your service quality remains high as your business grows. This could involve regular inspections, customer feedback, or staff training.
2. **Cost Management**: Keep a close eye on your costs as you scale operations. Look for cost efficiencies where possible, and monitor your spending carefully.
3. **Communication**: As your team grows, effective communication becomes even more important. Ensure that you have effective communication systems in place, and that all staff members are kept informed about important information.

Scaling operations is a crucial aspect of growth and expansion for a cleaning business. By understanding the importance of scaling operations, implementing effective scaling strategies, and managing the challenges of scaling, you can grow your business successfully while maintaining high service quality.

Exploring New Markets & Opportunities

Exploring new markets and opportunities is a key aspect of growth and expansion for a cleaning business. It involves identifying and pursuing new customer segments, geographic areas, or service offerings that can contribute to your business's growth. In this section, we will delve into strategies for exploring new markets and opportunities.

Understanding the Importance of Exploring New Markets and Opportunities

Exploring new markets and opportunities is important for several reasons:

1. **Diversification**: Diversifying your customer base or service offerings can reduce your business's dependence on a single market, making it more resilient to changes in market conditions.
2. **Increased Revenue**: New markets and opportunities can provide additional sources of revenue, contributing to your business's financial growth.
3. **Competitive Advantage**: Entering new markets or offering unique services can give you a competitive advantage, helping you stand out from your competitors.

Strategies for Exploring New Markets and Opportunities

Here are some strategies for exploring new markets and opportunities:

1. **Market Research**: Conduct market research to identify potential new markets or

opportunities. This could involve analyzing industry trends, surveying potential customers, or studying your competitors.
2. **Pilot Testing**: Before fully committing to a new market or opportunity, consider conducting a pilot test. This involves offering your services to a small segment of the new market to gauge its response and potential for success.
3. **Partnerships**: Forming partnerships with other businesses can provide opportunities to enter new markets. For example, you could partner with a property management company to offer your cleaning services to their clients.
4. **Innovation**: Innovate your service offerings to create new opportunities. This could involve offering new types of cleaning services, adopting new technologies, or finding new ways to deliver your services.

Managing the Challenges of Exploring New Markets and Opportunities

Exploring new markets and opportunities can bring challenges, such as unfamiliarity with the new market, increased competition, or the need for additional resources. Here are some tips for managing these challenges:

1. **Planning**: Plan your entry into new markets carefully. Understand the market's needs, competition, and cultural nuances. Develop a clear strategy for how you will attract and serve customers in the new market.

2. **Resource Management**: Ensure that you have the resources needed to explore new markets and opportunities. This could involve hiring more staff, investing in new equipment, or increasing your marketing budget.
3. **Risk Management**: Exploring new markets and opportunities involves risk. Manage this risk by conducting thorough market research, testing the market before fully committing, and being prepared to adapt your strategy as needed.

Exploring new markets and opportunities is a crucial aspect of growth and expansion for a cleaning business. By understanding the importance of exploring new markets and opportunities, implementing effective strategies, and managing the associated challenges, you can diversify your business, increase your revenue, gain a competitive advantage, and drive your business's growth.

Continuous Improve & Sustained Success

Continuous improvement and sustaining success in the long run are critical aspects of running a successful cleaning business. They involve constantly seeking ways to enhance your services, improve your operations, and adapt to changing market conditions. In this section, we will delve into strategies for continuous improvement and sustaining success in the long run.

Understanding the Importance of Continuous Improvement

Continuous improvement is a management philosophy that involves constantly seeking ways to improve your business's operations and services. Here's why continuous improvement is important:

1. **Enhancing Service Quality**: Continuous improvement can help you enhance the quality of your cleaning services, leading to higher customer satisfaction and loyalty.
2. **Increasing Efficiency**: By improving your processes and operations, you can increase efficiency, reduce waste, and lower costs.
3. **Staying Competitive**: Continuous improvement can help you stay competitive in the market. It allows you to keep up with industry trends, meet changing customer expectations, and stay ahead of your competitors.

Strategies for Continuous Improvement

Here are some strategies for continuous improvement:

1. **Customer Feedback**: Regularly seek feedback from your customers. This can provide valuable insights into how you can improve your services.

2. **Employee Training**: Provide regular training for your staff. This can help them improve their skills, stay updated with the latest cleaning techniques, and provide better service to your customers.
3. **Process Improvement**: Regularly review your business processes and look for ways to make them more efficient. This could involve adopting new technologies, eliminating unnecessary steps, or reorganizing your workflow.
4. **Benchmarking**: Compare your business with others in the industry. This can help you identify best practices, set performance standards, and find areas for improvement.

Sustaining Success in the Long Run

Sustaining success in the long run involves maintaining your business's performance over time, even as market conditions change. Here are some strategies for sustaining success:

1. **Adaptability**: Be adaptable. Be ready to adjust your strategies, services, or operations in response to changes in the market or customer expectations.
2. **Innovation**: Continually innovate your services and operations. This could involve offering new types of cleaning services, adopting new technologies, or finding new ways to deliver your services.
3. **Financial Management**: Manage your finances carefully. Ensure that your business

remains profitable, even as you invest in improvements or expansion.
4. **Customer Focus**: Stay focused on your customers. Understand their needs, meet their expectations, and strive to exceed them. This can help you maintain customer satisfaction and loyalty, even as your business grows and evolves.

Continuous improvement and sustaining success in the long run are crucial for the success of your cleaning business. By understanding the importance of continuous improvement, implementing effective improvement strategies, and focusing on sustaining success, you can enhance your service quality, increase efficiency, stay competitive, and ensure the long-term success of your business.

Chapter 11: Sustainability in the Cleaning Industry

Sustainability has become a key concern in all industries, and the cleaning industry is no exception. As awareness of environmental issues grows, there is increasing demand for cleaning services that are not only effective but also environmentally friendly. In this section, we will delve into the concept of sustainability and its importance in the cleaning industry.

Understanding Sustainability

Sustainability is about meeting our current needs without compromising the ability of future generations to meet their own needs. It involves balancing economic growth with the protection of natural resources and the environment. In the context of the cleaning industry, sustainability involves providing effective cleaning services while minimizing environmental impact.

The Importance of Sustainability in the Cleaning Industry

Sustainability is important in the cleaning industry for several reasons:

1. **Environmental Impact**: Traditional cleaning methods and products can have a significant environmental impact. They often involve the use of harsh chemicals that can pollute waterways, harm wildlife, and contribute to air

pollution. Sustainable cleaning methods aim to minimize these impacts.
2. **Health and Safety**: Many traditional cleaning products can also pose health risks to cleaning staff and building occupants. They can cause skin irritation, respiratory problems, and other health issues. Sustainable cleaning products are typically safer to use.
3. **Regulatory Compliance**: As awareness of environmental issues grows, regulations around the use of certain chemicals and waste disposal are becoming stricter. Adopting sustainable cleaning practices can help cleaning businesses comply with these regulations.
4. **Customer Demand**: More and more customers are seeking out businesses that prioritize sustainability. By offering sustainable cleaning services, cleaning businesses can attract these customers and differentiate themselves from their competitors.

Strategies for Sustainability in the Cleaning Industry

There are several strategies that cleaning businesses can adopt to become more sustainable:

1. **Green Cleaning Products**: Use cleaning products that are biodegradable, non-toxic, and made from renewable resources. These products can provide effective cleaning while minimizing environmental impact.

2. **Efficient Use of Resources**: Use resources efficiently. This could involve using less water and energy, reducing waste, and recycling wherever possible.
3. **Staff Training**: Train your staff on sustainable cleaning practices. This can help them understand the importance of sustainability and equip them with the skills to clean effectively while minimizing environmental impact.
4. **Sustainable Business Practices**: Beyond the cleaning services themselves, consider how you can make your overall business operations more sustainable. This could involve reducing energy use in your offices, choosing suppliers who prioritize sustainability, or offsetting your carbon emissions.

Sustainability is a crucial consideration for the cleaning industry. By understanding the importance of sustainability and implementing sustainable practices, cleaning businesses can reduce their environmental impact, improve health and safety, comply with regulations, and meet customer demand for sustainable services.

Green Cleaning Products

Green cleaning products are a cornerstone of sustainability in the cleaning industry. They are designed to minimize harm to the environment and human health, while still providing effective cleaning power. In this section, we will delve into the topic of green cleaning products and discuss their benefits.

Understanding Green Cleaning Products

Green cleaning products are cleaning agents that are designed to be environmentally friendly. They are typically made from natural ingredients, rather than synthetic chemicals, and are biodegradable, meaning they break down naturally in the environment. Green cleaning products are also typically free from harsh chemicals that can cause health issues, such as skin irritation or respiratory problems.

Benefits of Green Cleaning Products

The use of green cleaning products offers several benefits:

1. **Environmental Protection**: Traditional cleaning products often contain harsh chemicals that can pollute waterways and harm wildlife when they are washed down the drain. Green cleaning products, on the other hand, are made from natural ingredients that are biodegradable and less harmful to the environment.
2. **Health and Safety**: Many traditional cleaning products can cause health issues, such as skin irritation, eye irritation, and respiratory problems. Green cleaning products are typically gentler and safer to use.
3. **Effectiveness**: Despite being made from natural ingredients, green cleaning products can be just as effective as traditional cleaning products. They can effectively remove dirt,

grime, and bacteria, leaving surfaces clean and hygienic.

4. **Cost-Effective**: While some green cleaning products may be more expensive than their traditional counterparts, they can often be more cost-effective in the long run. They are often highly concentrated, meaning a small amount can go a long way. Additionally, the potential health benefits of using green cleaning products, such as reduced risk of health issues and allergies, can also result in cost savings.

Choosing and Using Green Cleaning Products

When choosing green cleaning products, look for products that are certified by a reputable environmental organization. This can help ensure that the products are truly environmentally friendly and safe to use.

When using green cleaning products, it's important to use them correctly to ensure their effectiveness. Follow the manufacturer's instructions for use, and remember that a little often goes a long way with these products.

Promoting Your Use of Green Cleaning Products

If your cleaning business uses green cleaning products, don't be shy about promoting this fact. Many customers today are environmentally conscious and prefer to do business with companies that share their values. Promoting your use of green cleaning products can help attract these customers and differentiate your business from your competitors.

Green cleaning products offer a way to provide effective cleaning services while minimizing harm to the environment and human health. By understanding green cleaning products and their benefits, choosing and using these products effectively, and promoting your use of green cleaning products, you can enhance your business's sustainability and appeal to environmentally conscious customers.

Energy-efficient Practices

Energy efficiency is a key aspect of sustainability in the cleaning industry. It involves using energy in the most productive way to deliver services, which not only reduces environmental impact but also results in cost savings for the business. In this section, we will delve into energy-efficient practices and their impact on the environment and the business.

Understanding Energy Efficiency

Energy efficiency refers to using less energy to perform the same task. In the context of the cleaning industry, this could involve using energy-efficient equipment, optimizing cleaning processes to use less energy, or implementing energy management practices in business operations.

The Importance of Energy Efficiency

Energy efficiency is important for several reasons:

1. **Environmental Impact**: Energy production often involves the burning of fossil fuels, which contributes to air pollution and climate change. By using energy more efficiently, a cleaning business can reduce its carbon footprint and contribute to environmental protection.
2. **Cost Savings**: Energy costs can be a significant expense for a cleaning business. Energy-efficient practices can reduce energy consumption, leading to substantial cost savings.
3. **Regulatory Compliance**: Increasingly, regulations are being introduced to encourage energy efficiency in businesses. Adopting energy-efficient practices can help a cleaning business comply with these regulations.
4. **Business Reputation**: A commitment to energy efficiency can enhance a business's reputation. It can demonstrate to clients and the public that the business is socially responsible and committed to sustainability.

Energy-Efficient Practices for a Cleaning Business

Here are some energy-efficient practices that a cleaning business can adopt:

1. **Energy-Efficient Equipment**: Use energy-efficient cleaning equipment. For example, choose vacuum cleaners, carpet cleaners, or pressure washers that are designed to use less energy.

2. **Optimized Cleaning Processes**: Optimize your cleaning processes to use less energy. For example, plan your cleaning routes to minimize travel time, or clean during daylight hours to reduce the need for artificial lighting.
3. **Energy Management**: Implement energy management practices in your business operations. This could involve monitoring your energy usage, setting energy-saving goals, and training your staff on energy conservation.
4. **Renewable Energy**: Consider using renewable energy sources, such as solar or wind power, for your business operations. This could involve installing solar panels on your business premises, or purchasing green energy from your utility provider.

The Impact of Energy-Efficient Practices

Implementing energy-efficient practices can have a significant impact on both the environment and the business:

1. **Environmental Impact**: Energy-efficient practices can reduce greenhouse gas emissions, contribute to cleaner air, and help mitigate climate change.
2. **Business Impact**: Energy-efficient practices can result in cost savings, compliance with regulations, and enhanced business reputation. They can also lead to improved operational efficiency and productivity.

Energy-efficient practices are a crucial aspect of sustainability in the cleaning industry. By understanding the importance of energy efficiency, implementing energy-efficient practices, and recognizing their impact, a cleaning business can reduce its environmental impact, save costs, comply with regulations, enhance its reputation, and contribute to a more sustainable future.

Chapter 12: Technology in the Cleaning Industry

Technology plays a pivotal role in the modern cleaning industry. It has transformed the way cleaning services are delivered, making them more efficient, effective, and environmentally friendly. In this section, we will delve into an overview of the role of technology in the cleaning industry.

Understanding the Role of Technology

Technology in the cleaning industry is multifaceted and impacts various aspects of the business:

1. **Cleaning Equipment**: Technological advancements have led to the development of more efficient and effective cleaning equipment. For example, high-efficiency particulate air (HEPA) filters in vacuum cleaners can trap a large number of very small particles that other vacuum cleaners would simply recirculate back into the air of your home.
2. **Cleaning Solutions**: Technology has also influenced the development of cleaning solutions. There are now products available that are not only more effective at cleaning but are also more environmentally friendly.
3. **Business Operations**: Technology also plays a significant role in the operational side of a cleaning business. From customer relationship management (CRM) systems that help manage client relationships, to automated scheduling

and invoicing systems, technology helps streamline operations, reduce manual work, and increase efficiency.
4. **Training**: Technology has revolutionized the way training is delivered in the cleaning industry. Online training platforms allow for ongoing education and the consistent delivery of training materials across various locations.

The Impact of Technology on the Cleaning Industry

The impact of technology on the cleaning industry is profound:

1. **Improved Efficiency and Effectiveness**: Advanced cleaning equipment and solutions enable cleaning tasks to be completed more quickly and effectively. This not only improves the quality of cleaning but also allows for more jobs to be completed in a day, increasing productivity and revenue.
2. **Enhanced Customer Satisfaction**: Technology helps improve the consistency and quality of cleaning, leading to enhanced customer satisfaction. Satisfied customers are more likely to become repeat customers and refer others to the business.
3. **Reduced Environmental Impact**: Many technological advancements in the cleaning industry have been geared towards reducing environmental impact. From green cleaning solutions to energy-efficient equipment,

technology is making it easier for cleaning businesses to be environmentally responsible.
4. **Streamlined Operations**: Technology helps streamline various business operations, reducing manual work, minimizing errors, and saving time. This allows business owners to focus more on strategic activities, such as business growth and customer relationship management.

Embracing Technology in the Cleaning Industry

Embracing technology is crucial for any cleaning business that wants to stay competitive in today's market. Here are some strategies for embracing technology:

1. **Stay Updated**: Keep up-to-date with the latest technological advancements in the cleaning industry. Attend industry events, subscribe to industry publications, and join industry associations.
2. **Invest in Technology**: Allocate a portion of your budget to invest in new technology. This could be new cleaning equipment, new software for managing your business, or new platforms for training your staff.
3. **Train Your Staff**: Ensure your staff are well-trained to use new technology. This will help maximize the benefits of the technology and ensure it is used effectively and safely.

Technology plays a crucial role in the cleaning industry, impacting everything from the cleaning process itself to how the business is managed. By understanding the role of technology, recognizing its impact, and embracing it, cleaning businesses can improve their services, streamline their operations, satisfy their customers, and stay competitive in the market.

Cleaning Technologies

The cleaning industry has seen a significant transformation with the advent of various high-tech cleaning solutions and cleaning robots. These technologies have not only improved the efficiency and effectiveness of cleaning services but have also introduced new ways to approach cleaning tasks. In this section, we will explore these technologies and their impact on the cleaning industry.

Cleaning Robots

Cleaning robots represent one of the most exciting advancements in the cleaning industry. These devices use a combination of sensors, artificial intelligence, and mechanical components to perform cleaning tasks autonomously. Here are some types of cleaning robots:

1. **Vacuum Robots**: These robots can navigate around a space, vacuuming as they go. They use sensors to avoid obstacles and can often be programmed to clean at specific times.
2. **Floor Scrubbing Robots**: These robots can scrub floors, making them ideal for cleaning

large floor areas such as in warehouses or supermarkets.
3. **Window Cleaning Robots**: These robots use suction to attach to windows and then clean them using built-in squeegees and cleaning solutions.

Benefits of Cleaning Robots

Cleaning robots offer several benefits:

1. **Efficiency**: Robots can work continuously without getting tired, allowing them to clean large areas efficiently.
2. **Consistency**: Robots can perform tasks with a high level of consistency, ensuring a uniform standard of cleanliness.
3. **Safety**: Robots can perform tasks that might be dangerous for humans, such as cleaning high windows.

High-Tech Cleaning Solutions

In addition to cleaning robots, there are also a variety of high-tech cleaning solutions that use advanced technology to improve the cleaning process. Here are a few examples:

1. **Ultrasonic Cleaning**: This technology uses ultrasonic waves to create microscopic bubbles in a cleaning solution. When these bubbles collapse, they produce a powerful cleaning action that can remove dirt and grime from surfaces.

2. **Electrolyzed Water**: This technology uses electricity to transform water and salt into a powerful, non-toxic cleaner and sanitizer. It's effective against a wide range of pathogens and is safe for use around people and pets.
3. **Microfiber Technology**: Microfiber cleaning tools use ultra-fine fibers to trap and remove dirt and bacteria. They can clean effectively with just water, reducing the need for harsh cleaning chemicals.

Benefits of High-Tech Cleaning Solutions

High-tech cleaning solutions offer several benefits:

1. **Effectiveness**: These technologies can often clean more effectively than traditional methods, removing more dirt and killing more germs.
2. **Safety**: Many high-tech cleaning solutions reduce or eliminate the need for harsh cleaning chemicals, making them safer for cleaning staff and building occupants.
3. **Sustainability**: Many high-tech cleaning solutions are more environmentally friendly than traditional methods. For example, they may use less water, produce less waste, or avoid harmful chemicals.

Cleaning robots and high-tech cleaning solutions are transforming the cleaning industry. They offer improved efficiency, effectiveness, safety, and sustainability, and are likely to play an increasingly important role in the industry in the years to come.

Digital Platforms & the Industry

Digital platforms and mobile applications have revolutionized the cleaning industry, transforming the way cleaning businesses operate and interact with their customers. In this section, we will delve into the impact of digital platforms and mobile applications on the cleaning business.

Understanding Digital Platforms and Mobile Applications

Digital platforms are online services that facilitate interactions between different users, such as businesses and customers. In the cleaning industry, digital platforms can connect cleaning businesses with potential customers, facilitate bookings, handle payments, and more.

Mobile applications, or apps, are software applications designed to run on smartphones and other mobile devices. Cleaning businesses can use mobile apps for a variety of purposes, such as managing bookings, communicating with customers, providing training for staff, and more.

The Impact of Digital Platforms

Digital platforms have had a significant impact on the cleaning industry:

1. **Increased Accessibility**: Digital platforms make it easier for customers to find and book cleaning services. Customers can compare different services, read reviews, and book a cleaning with just a few clicks.
2. **Efficient Operations**: Digital platforms can streamline operations for cleaning businesses. They can automate tasks such as scheduling, invoicing, and customer communication, saving time and reducing the risk of errors.
3. **Market Expansion**: Digital platforms can help cleaning businesses reach a larger customer base. By listing their services on a digital platform, businesses can reach customers beyond their local area.
4. **Customer Engagement**: Digital platforms provide opportunities for customer engagement. Businesses can interact with customers through reviews and messages, build relationships, and improve their services based on customer feedback.

The Impact of Mobile Applications

Mobile applications also have a significant impact on the cleaning industry:

1. **On-the-Go Management**: Mobile apps allow cleaning business owners and staff to manage their operations on the go. They can check schedules, communicate with customers, and access important information from anywhere.
2. **Real-Time Communication**: Mobile apps can facilitate real-time communication

between cleaning businesses and their customers. Customers can ask questions, make requests, or provide feedback, and businesses can respond promptly.
3. **Training and Resources**: Mobile apps can provide cleaning staff with training and resources. Staff can access training videos, cleaning checklists, safety guidelines, and more, right from their mobile devices.
4. **Marketing and Promotion**: Mobile apps can be used for marketing and promotion. Cleaning businesses can send notifications about special offers, share information about their services, and more.

Digital platforms and mobile applications are transforming the cleaning industry. They are making services more accessible to customers, streamlining operations for businesses, facilitating real-time communication, and providing valuable resources for staff.

Future Trends

The cleaning industry, like many others, is continually evolving with the advent of new technologies. Staying abreast of these changes is crucial for any cleaning business that wants to remain competitive and efficient. In this section, we will explore future technological trends in the cleaning industry and provide tips on how to stay updated.

Future Technological Trends in the Cleaning Industry

Several technological trends are set to shape the future of the cleaning industry:

1. **Advanced Robotics**: While cleaning robots are already in use, advancements in robotics and artificial intelligence are expected to make these machines even more efficient and versatile. Future cleaning robots may be able to handle more complex tasks, work in more varied environments, and even make autonomous decisions based on their surroundings.
2. **Internet of Things (IoT)**: The Internet of Things refers to the network of physical devices connected to the internet, collecting and sharing data. In the cleaning industry, IoT could enable cleaning equipment to communicate with each other and with a central system, optimizing cleaning schedules based on real-time data.
3. **Augmented Reality (AR)**: Augmented reality overlays digital information onto the physical world. In the cleaning industry, AR could be used for training purposes, guiding cleaners through tasks or showing them how to operate equipment.
4. **Green Technologies**: As sustainability becomes increasingly important, technologies that help reduce the environmental impact of cleaning are likely to become more prevalent. This could include more efficient cleaning

equipment, biodegradable cleaning products, and systems for reducing water and energy use.

Staying Updated with Technological Trends

Staying updated with these and other technological trends is crucial for any cleaning business. Here are some strategies for staying updated:

1. **Industry Publications**: Subscribe to industry publications, both online and offline. These publications often feature articles on the latest technological trends and how they're being applied in the cleaning industry.
2. **Trade Shows and Conferences**: Attend trade shows and conferences. These events often feature demonstrations of the latest cleaning technologies and offer opportunities to learn from industry experts.
3. **Online Research**: Regularly conduct online research. Many technology companies and industry organizations publish articles and white papers on the latest trends and advancements.
4. **Networking**: Network with other professionals in the cleaning industry. Sharing knowledge and experiences can be a valuable way of learning about new technologies.
5. **Training and Education**: Encourage ongoing training and education for yourself and your staff. Many training providers offer courses on the latest cleaning technologies and how to use them.

Technology is set to continue transforming the cleaning industry, making services more efficient, effective, and sustainable.

Chapter 13: Health and Safety Considerations

Health and safety considerations are paramount in the cleaning industry. Cleaning professionals are often exposed to various risks, including chemical hazards, physical injuries, and biological contaminants. In this section, we will delve into an introduction to health and safety considerations in the cleaning industry.

Understanding Health and Safety in the Cleaning Industry

Health and safety in the cleaning industry involve protecting cleaning professionals and the occupants of the premises being cleaned from potential hazards. These hazards can be categorized as follows:

1. **Chemical Hazards**: Cleaning professionals often work with cleaning products that contain potentially harmful chemicals. These can cause skin and eye irritation, respiratory problems, and other health issues.
2. **Physical Hazards**: Cleaning work can involve physical tasks such as lifting heavy objects, working at heights, or operating machinery, which can lead to injuries.
3. **Biological Hazards**: Cleaning professionals can be exposed to biological contaminants, such as bacteria, viruses, and fungi, especially when cleaning bathrooms, kitchens, or healthcare facilities.

The Importance of Health and Safety Considerations

Health and safety considerations are important for several reasons:

1. **Worker Protection**: Ensuring the health and safety of cleaning professionals is a moral and legal responsibility of cleaning businesses. It helps prevent injuries and illnesses, promotes worker well-being, and contributes to a positive work environment.
2. **Legal Compliance**: Cleaning businesses are required by law to provide a safe work environment and to comply with health and safety regulations. Failure to do so can result in legal penalties.
3. **Business Reputation**: A strong commitment to health and safety can enhance a cleaning business's reputation. It can demonstrate to clients and the public that the business is responsible and cares about its workers.
4. **Productivity and Quality of Service**: A safe and healthy work environment can contribute to higher productivity and better quality of service. Workers who are healthy and feel safe are likely to be more motivated and efficient.

Strategies for Ensuring Health and Safety

Ensuring health and safety in a cleaning business involves several key strategies:

1. **Risk Assessment**: Regularly conduct risk assessments to identify potential hazards and implement measures to control these risks.
2. **Training**: Provide regular health and safety training for your staff. This can help them understand the risks associated with their work and how to protect themselves.
3. **Personal Protective Equipment (PPE)**: Provide appropriate personal protective equipment, such as gloves, masks, and safety shoes, and ensure your staff know how to use them correctly.
4. **Safe Work Procedures**: Develop safe work procedures and ensure they are followed. This includes safe methods for lifting heavy objects, using cleaning chemicals, and operating cleaning equipment.

Health and safety considerations are a crucial aspect of running a cleaning business. By understanding the importance of health and safety, identifying potential hazards, and implementing effective health and safety strategies, cleaning businesses can protect their workers, comply with legal requirements, enhance their reputation, and improve their productivity and service quality.

Using Equipment Safely

The safe use of cleaning products and equipment is a critical aspect of health and safety in the cleaning industry. Cleaning professionals often work with a variety of cleaning products and equipment, each with its own potential hazards. In this section, we will delve into the safe use of cleaning products and equipment.

Understanding the Hazards of Cleaning Products and Equipment

Cleaning products and equipment can pose several types of hazards:
1. **Chemical Hazards**: Many cleaning products contain chemicals that can cause health problems if inhaled, ingested, or come into contact with skin. These can include irritation, allergies, burns, and in severe cases, poisoning.
2. **Physical Hazards**: Cleaning equipment can pose physical hazards. These can include cuts or punctures from sharp objects, burns from hot surfaces or steam, and injuries from heavy lifting or repetitive motions.
3. **Electrical Hazards**: Electrical cleaning equipment can pose a risk of electric shock, especially if used improperly or if the equipment is damaged.

Safe Use of Cleaning Products

Here are some guidelines for the safe use of cleaning products:
1. **Read and Understand Labels**: Cleaning product labels contain important information about the product's ingredients, hazards, and safe use. Always read and understand these labels before using the product.
2. **Use Appropriate Personal Protective Equipment (PPE)**: Depending on the

product, this may include gloves, goggles, aprons, or respiratory protection.
3. **Use Products as Directed**: Always use cleaning products as directed by the manufacturer. This includes using the correct amount of product, following any necessary safety precautions, and storing the product safely when not in use.
4. **Ventilation**: Ensure adequate ventilation when using cleaning products. This can help prevent the buildup of harmful fumes.

Safe Use of Cleaning Equipment

Here are some guidelines for the safe use of cleaning equipment:
1. **Training**: Ensure that all staff are properly trained in the use of cleaning equipment. This includes understanding the equipment's operation, safety features, and maintenance requirements.
2. **Regular Inspection and Maintenance**: Regularly inspect cleaning equipment and perform necessary maintenance to ensure it remains in safe working condition.
3. **Use Equipment as Directed**: Always use cleaning equipment as directed by the manufacturer. This includes using the equipment for its intended purpose, following safety precautions, and turning off and storing the equipment safely when not in use.
4. **Personal Protective Equipment (PPE)**: Depending on the equipment, PPE such as safety shoes, gloves, or hearing protection may be necessary.

The safe use of cleaning products and equipment is crucial for protecting the health and safety of cleaning professionals. By understanding the potential hazards of cleaning products and equipment, and by following guidelines for their safe use, cleaning businesses can prevent injuries and illnesses, comply with health and safety regulations, and create a safer working environment.

Work Environment

Maintaining a safe work environment is a critical aspect of health and safety in the cleaning industry. It involves creating conditions and practices that promote the safety and well-being of staff and clients. In this section, we will delve into strategies for maintaining a safe work environment for staff and clients.

Understanding the Importance of a Safe Work Environment

A safe work environment is important for several reasons:
1. **Employee Health and Safety**: A safe work environment protects employees from injuries and health issues. This can lead to lower absenteeism, higher job satisfaction, and higher productivity.
2. **Client Safety**: When cleaning services are performed at a client's premises, it's important to ensure the safety of the client and other occupants. This can enhance client

satisfaction and protect the cleaning business from liability issues.
3. **Regulatory Compliance**: Cleaning businesses are required by law to provide a safe work environment. Failure to do so can result in legal penalties.
4. **Business Reputation**: A strong commitment to safety can enhance a cleaning business's reputation. It can demonstrate to clients and the public that the business is responsible and cares about its workers and clients.

Strategies for Maintaining a Safe Work Environment

Here are some strategies for maintaining a safe work environment:
1. **Risk Assessment**: Regularly conduct risk assessments to identify potential hazards in the work environment and implement measures to control these risks.
2. **Safety Training**: Provide regular safety training for your staff. This can help them understand the risks associated with their work and how to protect themselves and others.
3. **Safe Work Procedures**: Develop safe work procedures and ensure they are followed. This includes safe methods for lifting heavy objects, using cleaning chemicals, operating cleaning equipment, and more.
4. **Personal Protective Equipment (PPE)**: Provide appropriate personal protective equipment, such as gloves, masks, and safety

shoes, and ensure your staff know how to use them correctly.
5. **Emergency Preparedness**: Prepare for emergencies by having a clear emergency plan, providing emergency training for your staff, and ensuring necessary emergency equipment, such as fire extinguishers and first aid kits, are available and easily accessible.
6. **Regular Monitoring and Improvement**: Regularly monitor your work environment and safety practices, and make improvements as necessary. This could involve regular safety inspections, soliciting feedback from your staff, and staying updated with the latest safety standards and best practices in the cleaning industry.

Maintaining a safe work environment is a crucial aspect of health and safety in the cleaning industry. By understanding the importance of a safe work environment, implementing effective safety strategies, and continually monitoring and improving your safety practices, you can protect your workers and clients, comply with health and safety regulations, enhance your business's reputation, and create a positive work environment.

Legal & Ethical Responsibilities

Understanding the legal and ethical responsibilities towards health and safety is crucial for any cleaning business. These responsibilities not only ensure the well-being of employees and clients but also protect the business from legal issues and enhance its reputation. In this section, we will delve into the legal and ethical responsibilities of a cleaning business towards health and safety.

Legal Responsibilities

Legal responsibilities refer to the obligations imposed on a cleaning business by laws and regulations. These responsibilities vary by location, but generally include the following:

1. **Providing a Safe Work Environment**: Cleaning businesses are legally required to provide a safe work environment for their employees. This includes ensuring that cleaning processes are safe, equipment is in good working condition, and employees are trained on safety procedures.
2. **Complying with Health and Safety Regulations**: Cleaning businesses must comply with all relevant health and safety regulations. These regulations may cover areas such as the use of chemicals, handling of waste, and use of personal protective equipment (PPE).
3. **Reporting and Record Keeping**: Many jurisdictions require businesses to report workplace accidents and illnesses to a government agency. Businesses may also be required to keep records of these incidents, as well as safety training and inspections.

Ethical Responsibilities

Ethical responsibilities refer to the obligations that a cleaning business has towards its employees, clients, and the community, based on moral principles and values. These responsibilities often go beyond legal requirements and can include the following:

1. **Prioritizing Employee Health and Safety**: Even in the absence of specific legal requirements, cleaning businesses have an ethical responsibility to prioritize the health and safety of their employees. This can involve providing safety training, using safer cleaning products, or implementing health and wellness programs.
2. **Protecting Client Health and Safety**: Cleaning businesses have an ethical responsibility to protect the health and safety of their clients. This can involve ensuring that cleaning processes do not leave harmful residues, maintaining client confidentiality, and respecting clients' properties.
3. **Contributing to a Healthy Community**: Cleaning businesses have an ethical responsibility to contribute to a healthy community. This can involve reducing environmental impact, participating in community health initiatives, or advocating for safer cleaning practices.

Balancing Legal and Ethical Responsibilities

Balancing legal and ethical responsibilities can be challenging but is crucial for the success and reputation of a cleaning business. Here are some strategies for balancing these responsibilities:

1. **Stay Informed**: Keep up-to-date with the latest laws, regulations, and ethical guidelines related to health and safety in the cleaning industry.
2. **Implement Best Practices**: Implement health and safety best practices in your business, even if they are not legally required. This can help you exceed legal requirements and meet ethical responsibilities.
3. **Promote a Culture of Safety**: Promote a culture of safety in your business. Encourage employees to prioritize safety, reward safe behavior, and create an environment where safety concerns can be openly discussed and addressed.

Understanding and fulfilling the legal and ethical responsibilities towards health and safety is crucial for any cleaning business. By staying informed, implementing best practices, and promoting a culture of safety, cleaning businesses can protect their employees and clients, comply with laws and regulations, meet ethical standards, and enhance their reputation.

Chapter 14: Building a Brand

Branding is a critical aspect of any business, including those in the cleaning industry. It involves creating a unique image and name for a product or service in the consumers' mind. In this section, we will delve into the importance of branding for a cleaning business.

Understanding Branding

Branding is more than just a logo or a tagline; it's the overall impression and experience that customers have when they interact with your business. It's about creating a distinct and lasting impression in the minds of customers. A strong brand can convey a company's values, tell its story, and create a sense of trust and reliability.

The Importance of Branding for a Cleaning Business

Branding is important for a cleaning business for several reasons:

1. **Differentiation**: The cleaning industry is often highly competitive, with many businesses offering similar services. A strong brand can help your business stand out from the competition and attract customers.
2. **Customer Recognition**: Having a strong brand makes it easier for customers to remember and recognize your business. When they need cleaning services, your business is likely to be the first one that comes to mind.
3. **Trust and Credibility**: A professional and consistent brand can help build trust and credibility with customers. It shows that your

business is established and reliable, which can make customers more comfortable in choosing your services.
4. **Customer Loyalty**: When customers have a positive experience with a brand, they're more likely to stick with it and become repeat customers. They're also more likely to recommend the brand to others, providing valuable word-of-mouth marketing.
5. **Employee Pride and Satisfaction**: Employees often feel more satisfied and motivated when they work for a well-branded company. A strong brand can instill a sense of pride and belonging among employees.

Building a Brand for Your Cleaning Business

Building a brand for your cleaning business involves several key steps:
1. **Understand Your Market**: Understand who your customers are, what they value, and what they expect from a cleaning service. This can help you create a brand that resonates with them.
2. **Define Your Brand**: Define what your brand stands for. What are your business's mission, values, and unique selling points? What kind of personality and tone do you want your brand to convey?
3. **Create a Visual Identity**: Create a visual identity for your brand, including a logo, color scheme, and typography. These should reflect your brand's personality and appeal to your target market.

4. **Deliver on Your Brand Promise**: Ensure that every aspect of your business, from your cleaning services to your customer service, delivers on your brand promise. Consistency is key in building a strong brand.
5. **Promote Your Brand**: Use various marketing channels, such as your website, social media, and print materials, to promote your brand and reach your target market.

Branding is a crucial aspect of running a cleaning business. By understanding the importance of branding, defining your brand, creating a visual identity, delivering on your brand promise, and promoting your brand, you can differentiate your business, attract and retain customers, build trust and credibility, and enhance employee satisfaction.

Selling Proposition & Brand Identity

Creating a unique selling proposition (USP) and a strong brand identity are crucial steps in building a brand for your cleaning business. These elements help differentiate your business from competitors and resonate with your target audience. In this section, we will delve into the process of creating a USP and brand identity.

Understanding Unique Selling Proposition (USP)

A USP is a factor or consideration presented by a seller as the reason that their service is different from and better than that of the competition. It's what your business stands for. It's the unique benefit or advantage that sets your cleaning business apart from others.

Creating a Unique Selling Proposition

Here are some steps to create a USP for your cleaning business:

1. **Understand Your Target Market**: Identify who your ideal customers are. What are their needs and pain points when it comes to cleaning services? What values and characteristics do they appreciate in a cleaning service?
2. **Analyze Your Competitors**: Understand what other cleaning businesses are offering. What are their strengths and weaknesses? How do they position themselves in the market?
3. **Identify Your Strengths**: What does your cleaning business do exceptionally well? This could be anything from specialized cleaning techniques, superior customer service, flexible scheduling, or environmentally friendly practices.
4. **Craft Your USP**: Based on your understanding of your target market, competitors, and your strengths, craft a USP that clearly communicates the unique value your cleaning business offers. It should be concise, memorable, and clearly differentiate your business from the competition.

Understanding Brand Identity

Brand identity is the visible elements of a brand, such as color, design, and logo, that identify and distinguish the brand in consumers' minds. It's the way you convey your brand to the world, including your logo, colors, typography, and imagery.

Creating a Brand Identity

Here are some steps to create a brand identity for your cleaning business:

1. **Define Your Brand Personality**: Is your brand modern or traditional, high-end or affordable, playful or serious? The personality of your brand should reflect your USP and resonate with your target market.
2. **Choose Your Visual Elements**: Choose the visual elements that will represent your brand, including your logo, color scheme, typography, and any other visual elements. These should reflect your brand personality and make your brand instantly recognizable.
3. **Create Brand Guidelines**: Create guidelines that specify how your brand's visual elements should be used. This includes when and where your logo can be used, what colors and fonts should be used in your marketing materials, and how images and graphics should be styled.
4. **Consistently Apply Your Brand Identity**: Apply your brand identity consistently across all touchpoints with your customers, including

your website, social media, advertising, and even the uniforms your cleaning staff wear. Consistency strengthens your brand and makes it more recognizable.

Creating a USP and brand identity are crucial steps in building a brand for your cleaning business. By understanding your target market and competitors, identifying your strengths, and consistently applying your brand identity, you can create a brand that stands out in the market, resonates with your customers, and drives the success of your business.

Graphic Design

Designing a logo and other visual elements of the brand is a critical step in building a brand for your cleaning business. These elements not only make your brand visually appealing but also communicate your brand's personality and values to your audience. In this section, we will delve into the process of designing a logo and other visual elements of the brand.

Understanding the Importance of a Logo and Visual Elements

A logo is a symbol or design that identifies your brand. It's often the first thing people see when they encounter your brand, and it can have a significant impact on their perception of your brand. Other visual elements of your brand, such as colors, typography, and imagery, work together with your logo to create a cohesive and appealing visual identity.

Designing a Logo

Here are some steps to design a logo for your cleaning business:

1. **Understand Your Brand**: Before you start designing, you need to have a clear understanding of your brand. What are your brand's personality, values, and unique selling proposition? Your logo should reflect these aspects of your brand.
2. **Look for Inspiration**: Look at the logos of other cleaning businesses, especially those that you admire or consider successful. What do you like about their logos? What don't you like? This can give you ideas and inspiration for your own logo.
3. **Sketch Your Ideas**: Start by sketching your ideas on paper. Don't worry about making it perfect at this stage; the goal is to get your ideas out of your head and onto paper.
4. **Refine Your Design**: Once you have a basic idea, you can start refining your design. Consider how it will look in different sizes and on different mediums. Make sure it's simple, memorable, and distinctive.
5. **Get Feedback**: Once you have a design you're happy with, get feedback from others. This could be your employees, customers, or a professional designer. Use their feedback to further refine your design.

Choosing Your Brand's Visual Elements

In addition to your logo, other visual elements of your brand are also important. Here are some tips for choosing these elements:

1. **Colors**: Choose colors that reflect your brand's personality. For example, green might be a good choice for a cleaning business that emphasizes eco-friendliness, while blue might be suitable for a business that wants to convey trust and reliability.
2. **Typography**: Choose fonts that are easy to read and reflect your brand's personality. For example, a modern, clean font might be suitable for a high-tech, innovative cleaning business, while a more traditional font might be better for a business that emphasizes reliability and trust.
3. **Imagery**: Choose images that reflect your brand's services and values. These could be photographs of your team at work, images of the results of your cleaning services, or illustrations that convey the benefits of your services.

Designing a logo and other visual elements of the brand is a crucial step in building a brand for your cleaning business. By understanding the importance of these elements, following a thoughtful design process, and choosing visual elements that reflect your brand's personality and values, you can create a visual identity that makes your brand stand out and resonates with your customers.

Online Presence & Reputation Management

Building a strong online presence and managing your reputation are crucial aspects of building a brand for your cleaning business. In today's digital age, most customers will interact with your brand online before they ever meet you in person. In this section, we will delve into strategies for building a strong online presence and managing your reputation.

Understanding the Importance of Online Presence

An online presence refers to the existence of an individual or business that can be found via an online search. The more platforms your business is connected to, the more robust your online presence. Here's why a strong online presence is important:

1. **Visibility**: Most customers turn to the internet to find and research cleaning services. A strong online presence makes it easier for potential customers to find your business.
2. **Credibility**: Having a professional-looking website and active social media accounts can enhance your business's credibility. It shows that your business is established and serious about its services.
3. **Customer Engagement**: The internet provides numerous opportunities for customer engagement. You can interact with customers through social media, respond to their queries via your website, and keep them updated with email newsletters.

Building a Strong Online Presence

Here are some strategies for building a strong online presence:
1. **Website**: Create a professional-looking website that provides information about your services, shares your unique selling proposition and brand identity, and offers a way for customers to contact you.
2. **SEO**: Implement search engine optimization (SEO) strategies to improve your website's ranking in search engine results. This can make it easier for potential customers to find your business.
3. **Social Media**: Establish a presence on social media platforms where your potential customers are likely to be. Share useful content, interact with your followers, and use these platforms to promote your services.
4. **Online Directories**: List your business in online directories. This can increase your online visibility and improve your website's SEO.
5. **Content Marketing**: Share useful content, such as blog posts or videos, that can help your potential customers. This can attract visitors to your website, enhance your brand's reputation, and improve your SEO.

Understanding Reputation Management

Reputation management involves monitoring and influencing how your cleaning business is perceived online. It involves managing both positive and negative content about your business and using strategies to enhance your reputation.

Managing Your Reputation

Here are some strategies for managing your reputation:

1. **Monitor Your Online Presence**: Regularly check what is being said about your business online. This includes reviews on your website and third-party sites, comments on your social media posts, and mentions of your business on other websites.
2. **Respond to Reviews**: Respond promptly and professionally to online reviews. Thank customers for positive reviews and address any issues raised in negative reviews.
3. **Manage Negative Content**: If you come across negative content about your business, address it promptly and professionally. This could involve resolving the issue with the customer, requesting that false information be removed, or sharing your side of the story in a respectful manner.
4. **Promote Positive Content**: Encourage your satisfied customers to share their positive experiences online. This could involve asking them to write a review, share a testimonial, or post about their experience on social media.

Building a strong online presence and managing your reputation are crucial aspects of building a brand for your cleaning business. By understanding the importance of online presence and reputation management, implementing effective strategies, and continually monitoring and improving your online presence and reputation, you can attract and retain customers, enhance your business's credibility, and build a strong brand.

Chapter 15: Dealing with Challenges and Setbacks

Running a cleaning business, like any other venture, comes with its own set of challenges and setbacks. These can range from operational issues to financial constraints, employee management, and customer satisfaction. In this section, we will delve into some of the common challenges and setbacks in running a cleaning business and provide insights on how to navigate them.

Operational Challenges

Operational challenges involve the day-to-day running of the business. These can include:
1. **Scheduling and Logistics**: Managing the schedules of multiple clients and employees can be a complex task. It involves coordinating the availability of staff with the needs of clients, managing travel times between locations, and adjusting schedules in response to unexpected changes or emergencies.
2. **Quality Control**: Ensuring consistent quality of service across different clients and locations can be challenging. It requires effective training and supervision of cleaning staff, implementation of quality control measures, and regular feedback from clients.
3. **Supply Management**: Keeping track of cleaning supplies and equipment, ensuring they are in good condition, and replenishing them when necessary is another operational challenge. Mismanagement of supplies can

lead to inefficiencies, increased costs, and reduced quality of service.

Financial Challenges

Financial challenges relate to the monetary aspects of running the business. These can include:
1. **Cash Flow Management**: Ensuring there is enough money to cover operational costs, pay salaries, and invest in business growth can be challenging, especially when clients delay payments or unexpected expenses arise.
2. **Pricing Strategy**: Setting prices that are competitive yet profitable is a delicate balance. Pricing too high can deter potential clients, while pricing too low can undermine profitability.
3. **Cost Control**: Keeping operational costs under control without compromising the quality of service can be challenging. It requires careful budgeting, regular monitoring of expenses, and making cost-effective decisions.

Employee Management Challenges

Employee management involves hiring, training, motivating, and retaining cleaning staff. Challenges in this area can include:
1. **Hiring and Training**: Finding reliable and competent cleaning staff can be difficult. Once hired, they need to be trained to deliver the standard of service your business promises.
2. **Employee Retention**: The cleaning industry often has a high turnover rate. Retaining good

employees requires providing competitive wages, good working conditions, and opportunities for growth and development.
3. **Employee Performance**: Ensuring all employees consistently perform at their best is another challenge. It requires regular performance evaluations, feedback, and coaching.

Customer Satisfaction Challenges

Customer satisfaction is crucial for the success of any cleaning business. Challenges in this area can include:
1. **Meeting Customer Expectations**: Customers may have high expectations for the quality of cleaning. Meeting these expectations requires understanding the customer's needs, providing high-quality service, and responding effectively to feedback.
2. **Building Customer Loyalty**: Encouraging customers to continue using your services over the long term requires building strong relationships, providing excellent customer service, and offering incentives for loyalty.
3. **Handling Complaints**: Dealing with customer complaints in a way that resolves the issue and maintains a good relationship with the customer can be challenging.

Running a cleaning business involves navigating various challenges and setbacks. By understanding these challenges, implementing effective strategies, and learning from setbacks, you can improve your business operations, financial management, employee management, and customer satisfaction.

Problem-Solving Strategies

Effective problem-solving is a critical skill for overcoming challenges and setbacks in running a cleaning business. It involves identifying problems, analyzing potential solutions, and implementing the most effective solution. In this section, we will delve into effective problem-solving strategies for running a cleaning business.

Understanding Problem-Solving

Problem-solving is a process that involves identifying a problem, generating and evaluating potential solutions, choosing the most effective solution, and implementing that solution. It's a critical skill for any business owner, as businesses often face a variety of challenges and setbacks that require effective problem-solving.

Problem-Solving Strategies

Here are some strategies for effective problem-solving in a cleaning business:

1. **Identify the Problem:** The first step in problem-solving is to clearly identify the problem. This involves recognizing that a problem exists and understanding what the problem is. For example, if your cleaning business is experiencing a high turnover rate among cleaning staff, the problem could be low job satisfaction, inadequate pay, or lack of opportunities for advancement.

2. **Analyze the Problem**: Once you've identified the problem, the next step is to analyze it. This involves gathering information about the problem, understanding its causes, and considering its impact on your business. For example, if the problem is low job satisfaction among cleaning staff, you might conduct surveys or interviews to understand why staff are not satisfied with their jobs.
3. **Generate Potential Solutions**: After analyzing the problem, generate a list of potential solutions. These should be realistic and feasible given your business's resources and constraints. For example, potential solutions to low job satisfaction might include increasing pay, providing more training, or improving working conditions.
4. **Evaluate Potential Solutions**: Evaluate each potential solution based on its feasibility, potential impact, and cost. Consider the pros and cons of each solution and how likely it is to solve the problem. For example, while increasing pay might improve job satisfaction, it would also increase costs and might not be feasible if your business is already struggling financially.
5. **Choose the Best Solution**: Based on your evaluation, choose the best solution. This should be the solution that is most likely to solve the problem, is feasible to implement, and provides the best balance of cost and benefit.
6. **Implement the Solution**: Once you've chosen the best solution, implement it. This

involves taking the necessary steps to put the solution into action, such as increasing pay, providing more training, or improving working conditions.
7. **Review the Outcome**: After implementing the solution, review the outcome. Has the solution solved the problem? If not, you may need to revisit the problem, generate new solutions, or try a different approach.

Effective problem-solving is a crucial skill for overcoming challenges and setbacks in running a cleaning business. By understanding the problem-solving process and applying effective problem-solving strategies, you can navigate challenges, improve your business operations, and enhance the success of your cleaning business.

Resilience & Overcoming Challenges

Resilience is a crucial trait for any business owner, including those in the cleaning industry. It refers to the ability to bounce back from setbacks, adapt to change, and keep going in the face of adversity. In this section, we will delve into the importance of resilience in overcoming challenges in running a cleaning business.

Understanding Resilience

Resilience is not just about surviving challenges and setbacks; it's about using those experiences to grow and improve. It involves maintaining a positive attitude, learning from mistakes, and developing coping strategies to deal with difficulties. Resilient business owners are able to navigate challenges, adapt to changes, and turn setbacks into opportunities for growth.

The Importance of Resilience in Overcoming Challenges

Resilience is important in overcoming challenges for several reasons:

1. **Business Longevity**: Running a business is a long-term endeavor filled with ups and downs. Resilience helps business owners weather the storms and keep going even when things get tough.
2. **Adaptability**: The business environment is constantly changing, with new competitors, technologies, and market trends. Resilience helps business owners adapt to these changes, seize new opportunities, and stay competitive.
3. **Problem-Solving**: Resilience enhances problem-solving skills. It encourages business owners to look at challenges from different angles, come up with creative solutions, and turn setbacks into opportunities.
4. **Employee Morale**: Resilient business owners can inspire their employees, foster a positive work environment, and lead their team through challenges. This can boost employee morale, productivity, and loyalty.

Building Resilience in Your Cleaning Business

Here are some strategies for building resilience in your cleaning business:

1. **Maintain a Positive Attitude**: Try to stay positive even in the face of challenges. This doesn't mean ignoring problems, but rather focusing on solutions and opportunities for growth.
2. **Learn from Mistakes**: Instead of dwelling on mistakes, use them as learning opportunities. Analyze what went wrong, how it can be avoided in the future, and what can be improved.
3. **Develop Coping Strategies**: Find healthy ways to cope with stress and adversity. This could involve physical exercise, meditation, or talking things over with a mentor or supportive colleague.
4. **Build a Support Network**: Surround yourself with supportive people who can provide advice, encouragement, and a fresh perspective. This could include mentors, fellow business owners, or a professional business coach.
5. **Plan for Setbacks**: Recognize that setbacks are a part of running a business. Have a contingency plan in place and set aside resources (like an emergency fund) to help you navigate through tough times.

Resilience is a crucial trait for overcoming challenges and setbacks in running a cleaning business. By understanding the importance of resilience, maintaining a positive attitude, learning from mistakes, developing coping strategies, building a support network, and planning for setbacks, you can navigate challenges, adapt to changes, and turn setbacks into opportunities for growth.

Positive Growth Mindset

Maintaining a positive mindset and learning from setbacks are crucial aspects of dealing with challenges in running a cleaning business. These elements not only help you navigate through difficult times but also contribute to personal growth and business success. In this section, we will delve into the importance of maintaining a positive mindset and learning from setbacks.

Understanding the Power of a Positive Mindset

A positive mindset is a mental and emotional attitude that focuses on the bright side of life and expects positive results. Having a positive mindset doesn't mean ignoring life's challenges. Instead, it's about approaching these challenges with a positive outlook, seeking solutions, and expecting success.

The Importance of a Positive Mindset

A positive mindset is important for several reasons:

1. **Resilience**: A positive mindset enhances resilience, helping you bounce back from

setbacks and keep going in the face of adversity.
2. **Problem-Solving**: A positive mindset opens your mind to new ideas, making it easier to find solutions to problems.
3. **Motivation**: A positive mindset can boost your motivation, helping you pursue your goals with enthusiasm and persistence.
4. **Stress Management**: A positive mindset can help you manage stress more effectively, reducing its impact on your health and well-being.

Cultivating a Positive Mindset

Here are some strategies for cultivating a positive mindset:

1. **Positive Self-Talk**: Pay attention to your self-talk. Try to replace negative thoughts with positive ones.
2. **Gratitude**: Practice gratitude. Regularly reflect on the things you are grateful for.
3. **Visualization**: Visualize success. Imagine achieving your goals and overcoming challenges.
4. **Mindfulness**: Practice mindfulness. Stay present and focused, rather than worrying about the future or dwelling on the past.

Learning from Setbacks

Setbacks are inevitable in any business. However, they can be valuable learning opportunities. Here are some strategies for learning from setbacks:

1. **Reflect on the Setback**: Take time to reflect on the setback. What went wrong? What could you have done differently?
2. **Seek Feedback**: Seek feedback from others. They may offer valuable insights and perspectives that you hadn't considered.
3. **Create a Plan**: Based on your reflections and feedback, create a plan to address the issue and prevent similar setbacks in the future.
4. **Implement the Plan**: Implement your plan. Monitor your progress and adjust the plan as necessary.

Maintaining a positive mindset and learning from setbacks are crucial for dealing with challenges in running a cleaning business. By understanding the power of a positive mindset, cultivating positivity, and learning from setbacks, you can navigate challenges, grow personally and professionally, and enhance the success of your cleaning business.

Chapter 16: Conclusion and Next Steps

In this book, we embarked on a comprehensive journey exploring the various aspects of running a successful cleaning business. Let's recap the key points discussed in each chapter:

Chapter 1: Introduction to the Cleaning Industry: We discussed the importance of the cleaning industry, its growth potential, and the various types of cleaning services. We also highlighted the benefits of starting a cleaning business, including low startup costs, high demand, and the ability to start small and expand over time.

Chapter 2: Starting a Cleaning Business: We explored the steps to start a cleaning business, including conducting market research, creating a business plan, obtaining necessary licenses and permits, purchasing equipment and supplies, and marketing your services.

Chapter 3: Business Operations: We delved into the operational aspects of running a cleaning business, such as scheduling, inventory management, quality control, and customer service.

Chapter 4: Hiring and Training Staff: We discussed the importance of hiring reliable and competent staff, providing effective training, and maintaining a positive work environment.

Chapter 5: Marketing and Advertising: We explored various marketing and advertising strategies, such as leveraging online platforms, utilizing print media, offering promotional deals, and building partnerships with local businesses.

Chapter 6: Customer Service Excellence: We emphasized the importance of excellent customer service in the cleaning industry, including understanding customer needs, exceeding expectations, handling complaints effectively, and building strong customer relationships.

Chapter 7: Financial Management: We discussed key aspects of financial management, including budgeting, pricing, managing expenses, and financial record keeping.

Chapter 8: Growth and Expansion: We explored strategies for growing and expanding a cleaning business, such as offering new services, targeting new markets, franchising, and building strategic partnerships.

Chapter 9: Sustainability in the Cleaning Industry: We highlighted the importance of sustainability in the cleaning industry, including using eco-friendly cleaning products, implementing energy-efficient practices, and promoting sustainability to customers.

Chapter 10: Technology in the Cleaning Industry: We delved into the role of technology in the cleaning industry, including the use of cleaning robots, high-tech cleaning solutions, digital platforms, and mobile applications.

Chapter 11: Health and Safety Considerations: We discussed health and safety considerations in the cleaning industry, including the safe use of cleaning products and equipment, maintaining a safe work environment, and legal and ethical responsibilities.

Chapter 12: Building a Brand: We explored the importance of branding for a cleaning business, including creating a unique selling proposition, designing a logo and other visual elements, building a strong online presence, and managing reputation.

Chapter 13: Dealing with Challenges and Setbacks: We discussed common challenges and setbacks in running a cleaning business, effective problem-solving strategies, the importance of resilience, and maintaining a positive mindset.

Running a successful cleaning business involves navigating various aspects, from starting the business, managing operations, hiring and training staff, marketing and advertising, providing excellent customer service, managing finances, planning for growth and expansion, embracing sustainability and technology, ensuring health and safety, building a strong brand, and dealing with challenges and setbacks.

Key Takeaways

In this comprehensive guide, we have explored the various aspects of starting and running a successful cleaning business. Let's highlight the most important takeaways that are crucial for your journey in the cleaning industry:

Starting a Cleaning Business: The first step towards running a successful cleaning business is to conduct thorough market research, create a detailed business plan, and obtain the necessary licenses and permits. Remember, starting small and expanding over time can be a viable strategy.

Business Operations: Efficient business operations are the backbone of a successful cleaning business. This includes effective scheduling, inventory management, quality control, and excellent customer service.

Hiring and Training Staff: Your staff is your most valuable asset. Hiring reliable and competent staff and providing them with effective training is crucial. Remember, maintaining a positive work environment can boost employee morale and productivity.

Marketing and Advertising: A well-planned marketing and advertising strategy can help you reach your target audience and attract more customers. Leverage both online platforms and traditional print media for a balanced approach.

Customer Service Excellence: Providing excellent customer service can set your business apart from the competition. Understand your customers' needs, exceed their expectations, and handle complaints effectively.

Financial Management: Sound financial management is crucial for the sustainability of your business. This includes effective budgeting, competitive pricing, managing expenses, and keeping accurate financial records.

Growth and Expansion: As your business stabilizes, consider strategies for growth and expansion. This could include offering new services, targeting new markets, or even franchising.

Sustainability in the Cleaning Industry: Embracing sustainability can give your business a competitive edge. Consider using eco-friendly cleaning products and implementing energy-efficient practices.

Technology in the Cleaning Industry: Leverage technology to improve efficiency and effectiveness. This could include using cleaning robots, high-tech cleaning solutions, digital platforms, and mobile applications.

Health and Safety Considerations: Ensuring health and safety in your business is both a legal and ethical responsibility. This includes safe use of cleaning products and equipment, maintaining a safe work environment, and understanding your legal and ethical responsibilities.

Building a Brand: A strong brand can set your business apart from the competition. Focus on creating a unique selling proposition, designing a memorable logo and visual elements, building a strong online presence, and managing your reputation effectively.

Dealing with Challenges and Setbacks: Running a business comes with its share of challenges and setbacks. Cultivate resilience, maintain a positive mindset, and see setbacks as opportunities for learning and growth.

Starting and operating a successful cleaning business involves navigating various aspects, from starting the business, managing operations, hiring and training staff, marketing and advertising, providing excellent customer service, managing finances, planning for growth and expansion, embracing sustainability and technology, ensuring health and safety, building a strong brand, and dealing with challenges and setbacks.

The Road Ahead

As we conclude this comprehensive guide on starting and running a successful cleaning business, it's important to look ahead and consider the future prospects of the cleaning industry. The road ahead is filled with potential opportunities for growth and expansion, but it also comes with its own set of challenges. In this section, we will discuss these aspects and provide insights on how to navigate them effectively.

Future Prospects of the Cleaning Industry

The cleaning industry has shown consistent growth over the years, and this trend is expected to continue. Several factors contribute to this positive outlook:

1. **Increased Awareness of Hygiene and Cleanliness**: The recent global health crisis has heightened awareness about the importance of hygiene and cleanliness, leading to increased demand for cleaning services.
2. **Advancements in Cleaning Technology**: Technological advancements, such as the development of more efficient cleaning equipment and the use of AI and robotics, are expected to drive growth in the cleaning industry.
3. **Sustainability Trends**: There is a growing trend towards sustainability and eco-friendly practices in all industries, including cleaning. Businesses that can offer green cleaning services are likely to have a competitive edge.
4. **Growth in Construction and Real Estate**: The growth in the construction and real estate sectors leads to increased demand for cleaning services for new buildings and properties.

Potential Opportunities for Growth and Expansion

Given these future prospects, there are several opportunities for growth and expansion in the cleaning industry:

1. **Diversification of Services**: Expanding your range of services to include specialized cleaning services, such as green cleaning, deep cleaning, or cleaning for healthcare facilities, can help attract a wider range of clients.
2. **Geographical Expansion**: Expanding your business to serve clients in new geographical areas can help increase your customer base.
3. **Franchising**: If your cleaning business model is successful, you might consider franchising. This allows others to start their own businesses using your brand and business model, leading to rapid expansion.
4. **Partnerships and Collaborations**: Forming partnerships or collaborations with other businesses can provide opportunities for growth. For example, you could partner with a property management company to provide cleaning services for their properties.

Challenges and How to Tackle Them Effectively

While there are many opportunities for growth and expansion, the road ahead also comes with challenges. Here are some potential challenges and strategies to tackle them effectively:

1. **Competition**: The cleaning industry is highly competitive. To stand out, focus on providing exceptional service, building a strong brand, and continuously innovating.
2. **Keeping Up with Technological Advancements**: As technology evolves, keeping up with the latest advancements can

be challenging. Invest in ongoing learning and development to stay updated with the latest trends and technologies.
3. **Maintaining Quality as You Grow**: As your business grows, maintaining the same level of quality can be challenging. Implement robust quality control measures and invest in training and development for your staff.
4. **Regulatory Compliance**: As you expand, you may need to comply with different regulations in different areas. Stay informed about the relevant regulations and ensure your business complies with them.

The road ahead for the cleaning industry is filled with opportunities for growth and expansion, but it also comes with challenges. By staying informed about industry trends, being proactive in seeking opportunities, and being prepared to tackle challenges, you can navigate the road ahead and continue to grow and succeed in your cleaning business.

Words of Encouragement

As we conclude this comprehensive guide on starting and running a successful cleaning business, it's important to take a moment to reflect on the journey ahead. Embarking on this entrepreneurial journey is a significant step, one that requires courage, determination, and a strong will to succeed. In this final section, we offer words of encouragement and motivation to inspire you as you embark on this exciting journey.

The Rewards of Running a Successful Cleaning Business

Running a successful cleaning business can be incredibly rewarding. It offers the opportunity to be your own boss, to create jobs, and to provide a valuable service to your community. It allows you to take control of your financial future and to reap the rewards of your hard work and dedication.

Moreover, a cleaning business is more than just a source of income. It's a chance to make a positive impact. Every day, you'll be improving the cleanliness and hygiene of homes and businesses, contributing to healthier and happier environments for people to live and work in.

The Power of Perseverance

The road to success is rarely smooth. There will be challenges and setbacks along the way. But remember, every challenge is an opportunity for learning and growth. Perseverance is your greatest ally on this journey. It's about having the resilience to keep going, even when things get tough.

When faced with a setback, take a step back and look at the bigger picture. Reflect on what went wrong and how you can avoid similar setbacks in the future. Use these experiences as stepping stones towards your ultimate goal.

Believe in Yourself

Believe in yourself and in your ability to succeed. You have the power to shape your own destiny. Your belief in yourself will be your guiding light, illuminating your path towards success.

Remember, self-belief isn't about ignoring your weaknesses or pretending that challenges don't exist. It's about acknowledging your strengths, embracing your potential, and having the confidence to tackle challenges head-on.

Stay Focused on Your Vision

Stay focused on your vision for your cleaning business. This vision is your roadmap to success. It's what guides your decisions and keeps you motivated when times get tough.

Your vision is unique to you. It's a reflection of your values, your aspirations, and your definition of success. Keep this vision at the forefront of your mind as you navigate your entrepreneurial journey.

Embrace Continuous Learning

Embrace continuous learning. The most successful entrepreneurs are those who are constantly learning and adapting. Stay curious, stay open-minded, and never stop learning.

Whether it's learning about new cleaning techniques, staying updated with industry trends, or improving your business skills, continuous learning will keep you at the top of your game.

In Conclusion

Embarking on the journey of starting and running a cleaning business is a bold and rewarding endeavor. It's a journey filled with opportunities for growth, learning, and personal fulfillment.

Remember, the road to success is a marathon, not a sprint. It requires patience, perseverance, and a positive mindset. But with determination and the right approach, you can navigate this journey successfully and build a thriving cleaning business.

As you embark on this exciting journey, remember the insights and strategies discussed in this book. They will serve as your compass, guiding you towards success in the cleaning industry. Here's to your success and the amazing journey ahead!

Final Thoughts

As we draw the curtains on this enlightening journey, it is essential to revisit the purpose of this book. The primary objective was to equip you, the reader, with the knowledge and tools necessary to start your own cleaning business. It is our hope that this book has served its purpose and has been a valuable guide on your entrepreneurial journey.

Starting a cleaning business, like any other venture, is a journey filled with challenges and opportunities. It requires dedication, hard work, and a clear vision. But with the right knowledge and tools, it can be a rewarding and profitable endeavor.

The chapters of this book have been carefully crafted to provide a comprehensive guide to starting a cleaning business. We started with the basics, understanding the cleaning industry, and identifying the opportunities it presents. We delved into the nitty-gritty of setting up a cleaning business, discussing aspects such as business planning, legal requirements, and financial management.

We explored the importance of marketing and customer service in building a successful cleaning business. We also discussed the significance of hiring and training staff, ensuring quality service delivery, and maintaining a healthy work environment.

As you embark on this journey, remember that the road to success is not always smooth. There will be obstacles and setbacks. But with perseverance and the right mindset, you can overcome these challenges and achieve your business goals.

Remember, every successful business started as an idea. The difference between success and failure often lies in the execution of that idea. This book has provided you with the knowledge and tools to execute your idea of starting a cleaning business. Now, it's up to you to take the next step.

Starting a business is a learning process. You will make mistakes, but each mistake is an opportunity to learn and grow. Don't be afraid to make mistakes. Instead, embrace them as part of your entrepreneurial journey.

Starting a cleaning business can be a rewarding and profitable venture. With the knowledge and tools provided in this book, you are well-equipped to start your own cleaning business. Remember, the journey of a thousand miles begins with a single step. Take that step today, and embark on your entrepreneurial journey.

We hope that this book has been a valuable resource on your journey to starting a cleaning business. We wish you all the best in your entrepreneurial endeavors. Remember, success is not a destination, but a journey. Enjoy the journey!

Thank you for choosing this book as your guide. We look forward to hearing about your success stories in the cleaning industry. Here's to your success!

www.ingramcontent.com/pod-product-compliance
Lightning Source LLC
Chambersburg PA
CBHW052158220526
45471CB00004B/1717